CAKE OR DEATH

The Excruciating Choices
of Everyday Life

HEATHER MALLICK

Alfred A. Knopf Canada

PUBLISHED BY ALFRED A. KNOPF CANADA

Copyright © 2007 Heather Mallick

www.randomhouse.ca

Library and Archives Canada Cataloguing in Publication

Mallick, Heather
Cake or death : the excruciating choices of everyday life /
Heather Mallick.

ISBN 978-0-676-97840-7

I. Title.

PN6331.M24 2007   c818'.6   C2006-905389-8

Text design: Kelly Hill

First Edition

Printed and bound in the United States of America

2 4 6 8 9 7 5 3 1

For my beloved, Stephen Petherbridge,
on whom I rely,
and
for Jennifer Allford,
the beautiful, the indomitable one.

"Planet Earth is an angry place; a searing bauble of rage. All this fury, roaring round the ether—and where does it go? The answer is it simply dissipates, flitters up toward the clouds, where it hangs around making pigeons sick and causing thunderstorms. Not good enough. We've got to work out a way of harnessing all this spare rage and using it to power our kettles. Come on, science. Hurry up. You wouldn't like us when we're angry."

—Journalist Charlie Brooker getting impatient,
The Guardian, 2006

"Life, she thought, is sometimes sad and often dull, but there are currants in the cake and here is one of them."

—from *The Pursuit of Love*, by Nancy Mitford, 1945

Contents

Introduction

Here, for your perusalment and enjoyage, is a collection of nice, shiny, all-new essays (for such was the insistence of my editor). I felt my older essays had mellowed and wised up—or is it wizened?—and were ready for drinking now. He thought not. Fine. Since when has a bottle of wine been left to age at my house anyway?

The reason I wanted to stick with my aging writing was that we live in awful times. Cruelty and stupidity flourish. We will look back on them with distaste, or worse, with nostalgia. So skip this era, I thought. It was not to be.

You'll detect some eccentricity, healthy I hope, nothing to frighten the horses, but an air of oddity, of slight unhingement. We Canadians are a stolid people, well-behaved to a fault. But I believe humans are all extraordinarily odd, and that's interesting. In life and in prose, it's good to inject a little strange.

I didn't come up with the title until long after Knopf had the *new! young! lustrous!* essays in its hands, and I can't claim it's entirely original. The choice between patisseries and the choir everlasting has long been a theme of British comedy, and British comedy has kept me going through the darker bits. I was watching a lot of Eddie Izzard stand-up comedy during a recent, fairly grim phase, and on *Dress to Kill,* he was talking bollocks, as he would put it, about how the Church of England wouldn't really be able to do fundamentalism with the élan of the Cathols, the Muslims, the more *excitable* religions. A Torquemada, for instance, would offer heretics painful death, no options. But the Vicar of Bray would offer fair-minded alternatives—death, or cake with a nice cup of tea.

Naturally, everyone would choose cake, and then the vicar would worry that they'd run out. And the parishioners wouldn't like it. "What, so my choice is 'or death'?" a lady dressed in a herbaceous border would say indignantly. "Well then, I'll have the chicken, please."

It's an eccentric set of alternatives, but an apt metaphor. For all that we are told that we lucky few in the

First World have infinite choice—in life itself, not to mention in track shoes and facial tissue—the choices are really quite stark. You have to figure out what life is, what your stance is on it and what version of yourself you find bearable. But you can see life as a blasted heath, a stark, waterless, comfortless, nasty place—and still narrow your eyes and pick out bits of cake. And if you do it right, you'll find there's a lot of cake about, in people's memoirs, for instance, in lovely taxes, in your own face even. Seek out things that give you pleasure; nobody else is going to do it for you.

I haven't had great deal of cake in my life, or so an American taught by the Declaration of Independence to pursue cake would say in utter mystification. I was raised in the Scottish manner, without pleasure. You don't accept compliments, you worry dreadfully about other people being poor (and cakeless) or treated in a way that is not nice, you feel terribly guilty about your new Gucci boots, and when you feel shamed about wanting to drag your husband to Paris when the man frankly prefers bucket-and-spade vacations, you have fits over whether you should go to Cuba. Yes, there's sun and sand, but how could you enjoy yourself knowing that only a short distance away, the Americans were torturing prisoners in Guantanamo?

When I have insomnia and try to put myself back to sleep with fantasies of winning a billion-dollar lottery, I dream of improving *maquiladora* factories. I would prefer to close them down but I have a responsibility to my employees. So I improve conditions. There I lie till dawn breaks, planning a new ventilation system and a green roof for my factories. In the end, I arise for a day that is less tiring than my nighttime fantasies.

At this point, I usually say, "Screw this, we're going to Paris." So I go and drink wine and eat *boudin* for breakfast. I don't loll or stroll or ponder or even *fais du lèche-vitrines*, I shop in the Napoleonic fashion—I must have this, and I must have it now, although it is very cold on the way to Moscow and I will die but still—and I throw myself into pleasure. As the essayist Nora Ephron puts it, do you splurge or do you hoard? I do both, with much angst. I love my husband—whom I chose instantly out of the very sorry lineup that is men—I love my girls, I live for books and friends, and the world is so full of a number of things, from cabbages to kings, all of it within my reach.

You'll think the book has little to do with cake, but you would be wrong. Clearly, the essays are mostly slanted on the side of death, but may I say that the last one is a real piece of cake. So there. You can splurge *and* hoard. You can enjoy *and* give plentifully to others. You can choose cake *and* death.

Mrs. Tittlemouse

Why we clean, an essay to grease the elbows

 I am so bloody
depressed. And the awful thing about it is that gloom used
to be something to be ashamed of. I was very good at being
ashamed of it and had a variety of slogans to use as cricket
bats on my head. "Just get on with it" was one. "Mustn't
grumble" was another. Until I realized that I was earning a
fine income doing just that, that is, writing newspaper
columns that were essentially me grumbling for 850
words every week. "Just do it" was very good, the only
thing for which Nike deserves credit.

But the slogans don't work any more. Stephen Fry once wrote that just as they have laugh tracks on television comedies, so should they have weeping tracks on the news. And he wrote that during the *first* Gulf War and he hadn't even had his nervous breakdown, which culminated in him sitting in a car in Bruges contemplating the other use for an exhaust pipe.

There isn't anything on the news to cheer anyone. One response would be to stop watching it, but look what happened to the United States when the citizens of that huge once-rich-now-debtful-I-just-don't-know-what-to-do-with-myself country stopped paying attention. The place exploded, then imploded, and bits started falling off, like New Orleans soon followed by the rest of Louisiana. In 2004, the nadir was reached after George W. Bush's second alleged election. An American student was reduced to setting up a website called sorryeverybody.com and stacks of smart Americans rigid with shock and coated with pessimism sent in pictures of themselves holding up signs apologizing to the world.

I cried as I watched it online, but by 2004 I was crying pretty easily.

The trough of melancholy in which we live now is a shallow grave. My husband, whom we shall call S., is British and doesn't understand the concept of depression. Every day spent outside his homeland is a holiday, according to him. When I tell him how sad I am, he asks why. Foolishly, I tell him. There's an awful phrase about how you have to "take things on board," meaning hear them and live with them. Clearly, I cannot take things on board. Because I tell S. that these men called the Janjaweed are kidnapping children in the Sudan and . . .

S. is humane. He understands the wrongness of the Janjaweed but does not grasp why I am devastated by the wrongdoing of mad people in a faraway country not only of which I know nothing but that I can't even pick out of an atlas. We know this because he has brought an atlas into the bedroom where I am curled.

"You know that song 'Every Little Thing You Do Is Magic'?" he says. I nod, but don't rise to this as I know he hates Sting. Presumably because Sting is a Brit who still finds a reason to live in Britain and is a prat and poseur. "If you were writing that song," he says, "it would go, *'Every little thing you do is rubbish.'*"

He laughs. I don't.

I think I know why we are still conjoined. We couldn't be more different. I like this. I wish I were him. We were watching the Springsteen tribute to Pete Seeger the other day and he, who loathes hip hop, said, "The progress of American music—from Hoedown to Down, ho." And he sat there grinning at his own cleverness. I wish I could come up with lines like that. But I am gloomy, and somehow I admire the fact that my deep gloom is a source of amusement to him. (On the other hand, he doesn't understand North American ethical laxity. The other day in a seafood restaurant, he actually said to me, "Why did you order that if you weren't going to finish it?" Seriously. "I guess it just worked out that way," I said.)

Anything can set me off. In 2004, I felt so desperately sorry for Blue State Americans, those nice people, a credit to a nation that was about to go all excremental. And there's no going back, they realized that, and on that website, they sent out telegrams of shame and sorrow, a student dorm arranging their apology in the form of track shoes, people's babies holding up signs (I normally disapprove of this—your baby has no opinions on stem cells, lady—but those babies were going to grow up with the consequences). You poor kid. Some blue-eyed Democrat guy in Texas looked grim, saying he had voted behind enemy lines, and he might as well have been a Resistance fighter in France in the Second World War, sending a coded message on his little radio hidden in a baguette.

An American tourist in Canada visiting what looked like Lake Louise wrote "I'm sorry you have to live next door to us" and my face got all crumply and wet, like a sodden piece of paper towel. Then Canadians accidentally voted a bit too right-wingly and I felt sorry for that young woman in retrospect. She no longer had us as her hideout. We were Narnia full of goofballs, and suddenly we were mean goofballs with bellies crawling with complaints.

You really do need a sound FX machine for the news now. The soundtrack for *Deliverance* could play whenever an Abu Ghraib story came up. Now those toothless backwoods boys had jobs. Cue a needle-like scream for Madeleine Albright smugging about how the deaths of half a million Iraqi children under UN sanctions were fine with her, and a chunky spew for any Scientologist. Cue the nightmare zither from *The Third Man* while watching Tony Blair's crusty little teeth growing down to his toes as he told his lies from the pulpit. Or maybe everyone would be automatically naked and you could comfort yourself with how bad all forked animals looked compared to the pelted ones they were driving out of existence.

But these would be panaceas, mere toys. I didn't need that. I needed something stronger than religion. It was a craving for order. Now I know what you're thinking—this is where Germany ran into trouble in the 1930s—but I didn't mean public order. I meant personal order. Something much more benign and mine own.

I became Mrs. Tittlemouse. Beatrix Potter doesn't rate highly as literature by people who judge such things, but they are wrong. She is heaven in a sponge mop. I read her as a child and to this day love her paintings, her stories, her home-boiling of squirrels so her watercolours could be anatomically exact. Beatrix Potter made domesticity desirable.

All right, she didn't, but she domesticated me. Personal order has become my badge and the only thing that really works for depression.

I'm not saying it makes you un-depressed. You're still hideously depressed but you're a hideously depressed person who has ironed all her sheets and made a fine bed with hospital corners and highly placed blankets with a generous chin of linen. It's nothing to sneer at. It's an accomplishment and depressed people don't have many of those.

Neither do cheerful people these days (or is that just me and my green unhealthy glow of gloom?).

My side of the street has been cleared of litter by my own hands, and I don't care if it looks odd. I think it looks . . . tidy. I would have said it looked Dutch, but the Dutch went a bit racist recently so the Keukenhof will have to bloom this spring without me. Very few places on the planet left to visit with a clear conscience, I note.

Tidiness didn't register with me when I was young. It doesn't register with adults now. For instance, I doubt smokers can be trained to think of cigarette butts as litter even though the orange stubs lie stained, flattened and oddly curled outside the bus shelter like a covey of maggots. The butts, I mean. In a smoker's mind, the ciggie is over and the butt does not rate as an object.

I understand this. I leave the butts where they lie. But when I walk up my street to the Chinese restaurant with its excellent free wings with orders over $30 or to the pharmacy with those nice sensible people in their white smocks giving me pretty little pills for what ails me, I pick up litter for the bin at the end of the road. Not for houses with Conservative signs—they will rely on market forces—but everyone else can wonder where that rotting pack of McDonald's fries that sat in the front lavender bed for a month disappeared to. Not down their dog's throat but into the garbage.

I vacuum with my German-made Miele. It has a HEPA filter which means that what goes in stays in. I use it for dusting too, although I sometimes forget to turn the suckage down and the thing eats badly chosen paint from the radiator covers (you need a primer if you use latex over oil, Dodgy Bros. Painters). Then I look at the carpet and it is fleckless. I am not fleckless. I am depressed. But you can't quarrel with a blank-faced expanse of carpet. One part of it is like any other. There's something lovely, something reliable, about that.

Should the worst happen, a bad oyster perhaps, you can lie on that carpet and think, as I have, that it's not the worst place in the world to die slowly. I've vomited in Moscow subway toilets and Paris department stores and I've gotten to know the bogs quite well, their shapes, their reliable coldness, their antiseptic smell. But the floors on which I knelt have been as a stranger to me. You don't know who they've had as guests. Why the bogs should be so clean is a pleasant mystery. Of course they're only surface-clean. I remember my high school biology teacher, Mr. Liptak, sending us with petri dishes and agar into corners of our high school, including the wash-rooms, to let the dishes do nothing more than sit. We'd bring the empty glass containers back and watch the stuff starting to grow, beige eternal matter that looked inerad-icable. How could you scrub every corner of every room so that nothing would sprout? Despite our complaints, we know doctors are not wrong nowadays to eject us from hospitals the day after the operation. Without a private room and utterly manic cleanliness from personnel in white impermeable suits, the beige stuff is coming for us.

I regard my last Moving Day with disbelief. It's part of the reason why I have sunk money into this small house. I cannot contemplate a moving day again. That day was a sinkhole, and it's my fault. I picked out of the Yellow Pages the worst moving company in existence. By the end of moving day, they had broken so much furniture that they owed me money.

But the worst thing was the chunky guy who went into the bathroom and began, how can I put this, a good clear-out. He must have been in there for a half-hour. It was a brass band of wind-breaking, a prolonged trumpeting of such volume that eventually none of us could pretend it wasn't happening because it was drowning out the conversation. Even his workmates were embarrassed and told him enough was enough. "Hey, I gotta go," he shouted back. It sounded like the Grade Four class at your kid's school doing a tuba version of "God Save the Queen."

A week later, at the freshly renovated house, I opened the box containing my vacuum cleaner. A foul odour rose out of it, like liquefied hyena. Somehow that man's inner atmosphere had been packed and moved. I didn't know you could transport air in an unsealed box, and this has changed my attitude to a lot of things.

Every evening now I light a Lampe Berger, a catalytic converter that burns scented "ozoalcohol," killing bacteria and making the house smell like gardenias. It's pleasant, and no one asks me why I do it. Which is lucky as I'd have to explain that I have never recovered from the revelation of the packaging possibilities of hell smells.

A house will always be a beacon for bacteria. I will never forget that news story out of Japan headlined "Underwear a nest for ringworms." Doctors were warning citizens about their national habit of wearing underpants to bed. Air, sunlight, cleanliness! What can I do to regulate this mad microscopic world?

Here come the stripes.

Over the years I have straightened out in the decorating sense. I look at my living room now, with the broad yellow-and-white striped Roman blinds, the radiators, bleached parallel oak stair rails, the indents on the white-painted wood of the fireplace surround, the evenly loaded and staggered bookcases, and I realize with both pleasure and embarrassment that the theme of my house is stripes. Straight lines. Yes, there are blots of colour like the Julia McNeely painting of the red rooster and the mini-explosion of book dust jackets, but anyone with an eye could come into this house and see a regimented, possibly disturbed mind.

Okay, so it's not normal. (But how I hated that designer who suggested removing all dust jackets so that books would be a uniform beige and thence a calming silent witness to a sand-coloured life? What an attractive red splatter her blood would make against my library.)

I like things in rows. It comforts me. It's not necessarily wrong to be comforted by order. But rows? You know what the ultimate row is? The bars of a jail cell. I have muntin bars, those internal faux grilles that make the windows easy to clean. My house is filled with racks and levels, stairs and shelves; with linage, both perpendicular and horizontal. It is choked with symmetry. And outside, garden trellis—that's magnificent.

No, it is not normal. I rarely have anyone over unless they're understanding types.

Also there's a lot of softness in the house, velvet, brushed cotton, fringes, cushions. Am I just shoving this fact in to hide something Teutonic, not a passion for order and straight lines, but a mania? Why am I never on time for appointments but always ten minutes early? Since I often hear from lunatics and frequently get drunken e-mails and phone calls from my odd bosses or readers, I have to keep records. I keep a hard copy and place it in a file labelled Loonies. These crazies are filed, they're under control, even though they're still out there with their little brains boiling.

And it isn't superficial. It goes to the core. I was as horrified as anyone when Barbara Ehrenreich went undercover at one of those franchised Jolly Maid Services and discovered that they tidy and make everything look sparkling, but they don't really clean. They don't even have Miele vacuums. The microscopic flakes of human skin that make up dust, they just disperse. To where? Imagine oiling the kitchen sink to make it gleam without having Vim-ed the thing first.

There was a time when this wouldn't have bothered me, but the world wasn't so chaotic then. What would Mrs. Tittlemouse have said?

We can check, thanks to Beatrix Potter.

Mrs. Tittlemouse was a woodmouse and she lived in a bank under a hedge. Cozy doesn't begin to describe it. There she is at her tiny door (not quite tiny enough as we shall discover when Mr. Toad squeezes in) in a pink and white striped dress (stripes again) under a large white apron. She's quite a stout fireplug of a person. I am slender, nay bony, but I think stoutness should be more prized, the way it was at the turn of the century when a certain roundness implied prosperity and a level of jollity. Such a funny little house! thinks Mrs. Tittlemouse. It's full of nooks and crannies. Speaking as someone who despises John Pawson—the minimalist king who brought us grey rooms furnished with armless grey chairs, grey stone coffee tables with an oddly shaped grey bowl sitting on them, and little else (he doesn't "do" bookshelves, too frolicsome)—I like the Tittlemouse look, oh I do. She has a kitchen, parlour, pantry, larder, and a bedroom with a little box bed. One day I'll sleep in a box bed.

She is always sweeping and dusting, much like me, although she is a mouse and I am a woman who likes lying on the couch and reading and calling out for more wine. She doesn't like insects with their dirty feet, spiders with their nasty cobwebs and bumblebees who enter without permission—as if they'd ever be given it—and set up house in piles of moss, buzzing alarmingly at their hostess.

Filthy drippy old Mr. Jackson the amphibian is allowed to stay for dinner because Mrs. Tittlemouse is polite, but there's method in her hospitality. He eats creepy-crawlies hiding in the plate rack, scares away butterflies in the sugar bowl and positively exterminates bees.

But this is where the story gets exciting. When everyone has been eaten or has left and Mrs. Tittlemouse is alone with honey smears, muddy footprints and God knows what on the crockery. This is the life of everyone with a house. Mrs. Tittlemouse is terribly upset by the mess. She has a task and sets herself at it in a way that makes it clear that tidiness and cleanliness sit up straight within her very soul.

She spring-cleans for a fortnight. No Swiffering. She scrubs, she soaps, she dusts and rubs and polishes. And then the place gleams and a peaceful softness steals over Mrs. Tittlemouse's heart. The sheets she tucks into her box bed are clean and fragrant. It's the same feeling Yeats had when he arose and went to Innisfree to plant nine bean rows. It's that pause when the poet W.H. Davies stands and stares. It's that fine feeling a woman gets when her words are completed on the page and the publisher's cheque is swallowed by the ATM and the dollars will flow to become fine garments and C.P. Cavafy's sensual perfumes of every kind, flights to distant cities and swellings in the coffers of universities her daughters earnestly wish to attend so as to learn from their scholars.

But her home is gleaming and her perennial beds are well-mulched with mushroom compost and all is well in this one plot of fertile, chemical-free land in a world where the news should come with a wailing track. And it would too, but we're too embarrassed to admit what a failure we are as a species.

So I hug my blues to myself—I knew I could count on you, blues, grim companion of my middle years—and I tend my own place and I follow the wise and wonderful Mrs. Tittlemouse and that's all we can achieve. It's small, it's less than small. But it will have to do. The freakish housecleaning expert Cheryl Mendelson says a well-kept house is one that you enter and find nothing needs be done. It is waiting for you. The theorist-of-everything Alain de Botton says more nobly that we come home each workday from a world of insincerity, envy, bureaucracy, and squandered time to a place that reflects our "authentic selves." There is gentleness, he says, in the softness of our curtains. For the first time I wonder why fabric is shunned in offices. Clackety plastic blinds are favoured, when in fact, curtains are easier to clean.

Little art there is that celebrates cleaning. Kate Bush's 2005 CD *Aerial* has a song, "Mrs. Bartolozzi," presumably about a housekeeper, on a rainy Wednesday when people traipsed mud through the house and how it had to be scrubbed out of the hall carpet. Then comes the joy of collecting all the dirty linens in the wash basket and putting them in the washing machine. *"Washing machine"* sings Kate. Her blouse wraps around her husband's trousers, slishy sloshy, and it is as if she has walked into the ocean with her skirt floating around her and little fish swim between her legs.

When I need calming, I watch the front-loader throwing clothes, around, back and forth, with a slappy sound. And then the waves come in and the soap froths against the glass. It is sublime.

It hasn't been quite as sublime since the machine attacked me. It has a little pullout drawer into which you pour detergent concentrate. Since I had opened a new jug, some blue liquid spilled onto the carpet. I grabbed a rag and started mopping up. Then I stood up suddenly, hit the edge of the pullout drawer, and crashed to the ground, listening to myself with interest for I seemed to be screaming with pain. The gash in my head bled for three hours. Painkillers and wine . . . should have been a country song. Then clear liquid began coming out of the wound. On the off-chance that it was brain juice and not plasma, I licked it off my fingers. It was bland.

I cannot move to Japan and join one of its cleaning communes, but I read about them and something calls out to me. Louise Rafkin, an American housecleaner who wrote a fine book called *Other People's Dirt: A Housecleaner's Curious Adventure,* taught me about a man named Tenko-san who in the late 1800s decided that work was a way of giving thanks for life. So he worked and cleaned for others as a way of offering a pure thanks. Today about 150 people remain in the group he founded.

When I heard that Japan has a national Day of Labour, in which everybody cleans, I was lovestruck. My city holds a clean-up day on April 22nd on which nobody does a damn thing. I want to see everyone out on the street with their special see-through green garbage bags, but it's just me alone grubbing in my neighbours' shrubs for condoms and the cellophane wrappers from cigarette packages. Even if I'm the one plucking their debris, I can only congratulate smokers for getting to their drug. Shrink wrap is the bane of my existence.

Rafkin is my kind of woman. She tells us the Japanese words for different kinds of dirt and I go into a semi-aroused state. I am excited by dirt only in that I envision cleaning it up. *Gicho-gicho* means "dripping with grease" but *gucho-gucho* just refers to a jumble. *Nuru-nuru* means "slimy." *Gyogan* is humble toilet-cleaning. Why call it humble? You get important psychological rewards from cleaning a toilet. Windexing a mirror hardly provides the same shot of gratification.

I once cleaned my stepdaughter's kitchen. It wasn't her dirt but the dirt of male roommates and there was ooze and insectry, odour and food that wouldn't move, ketchup dried on the tip of the bottle like blackened foreskin, as Bruce Robinson wrote in *Withnail and I*. She howled with delight when she saw the results, and embraced me tearfully. I could not tell if it was joy at such a revelation of love from a stepmother (we are reputed to be evil; I, however, would eat *gicho-gicho* to earn my stepdaughters' love) or at being related to an unofficial member of a Japanese cleaning cult.

And so I count few people as my friends. I trust almost no one wholly. I am convinced of my husband's love and extend a hand to any stranger. But I am in a trough of melancholy, like a wet trench in the First World War. It isn't pleasant and requires an enormous effort of will to keep going each day. But mine is the tidiest, coziest, most fetching trench on the Maginot Line, and for that I thank my alter ego Mrs. Tittlemouse.

Tell Me Where It Hurts

*In which we learn and yet take some
pleasure from the pain of others*

 This is the era
of the Pain Memoir. Presumably these books will continue selling until humans stop suffering pain. Fat
chance, eh?

I remember a writer being sneered at by a reviewer
for unconsciously sending out the message that "novels
are how-to books for living." I was bewildered and
annoyed. Because *of course* novels are how-to books for
living. Why else would anyone write them or read them?
Novels help you articulate the struggles of your own life

and, at the very least, tell you what not to do. That Vronsky, he's trouble, for instance.

But biographies, autobiographies and memoirs are best of all. Stuff happened. Memoirs are infinite in their griefs and oddities and yet by definition (she lived to write the book), the author has survived. And they're a grab bag. Yes, you have Eisenhower trying to decide which day would have the most favourable weather for the Normandy invasion. But his wartime lover, Kay Summersby, wrote equally interestingly about their awkward efforts to have sexual intercourse without anyone suspecting. She remembers her silk underthings, intended to entrance the general. They failed. He was impotent, presumably had weather on his mind.

Great events and personal limpness, it's all part of the memoir genre.

That is why the scandal about that American, James Frey, trying very hard to have lived a shocking life, is significant. He wrote a memoir—which I shan't bother to read—of my favourite kind. He was miserable and drug-addicted; lots of tooth loss and some of it by his own hands (or was that from a parody after the scandal?), wet black American freeway stuff, life on the grotty edge, plenty of skanks, jolly good. I enjoy curling up in a highly stuffed sofa under a blankie and reading about the sufferings of others. It isn't that I take joy in it. But I've suffered, just like every other human, in my own special, dull way, and it comforts me to read that I am not alone, despite not having spent time in Japanese prisoner of war camps. And furthermore, they lived to tell the tale so that's all right then. No, I have never read *The Diary of Anne Frank*. I draw the line at the misery of children who didn't survive to hide it from their own children.

James Frey suffered mentally and physically. Apparently, he was torn, figuratively, into a million little pieces. Except he wasn't. He made a lot of it up. And thus his agent, editor, publisher and, sadly, every reader of his novel has now learned not to quite trust anything in the memoir genre. This isn't good, not only because people telling the truth about their lives has improved our own flawed lives and selves so much, but because readers will turn to fiction again. And 95 percent of North American fiction is unspeakably bad (75 percent for Brits), which destroys the capacity of reading in later life to compensate for appalling schools.

Lies have increasingly snuck their way into autobiographies and memoirs (not biographies, for their accuracy is a biographer's lifeblood. Or perhaps it's more of a status thing.) The reason is what the comedian Stephen Colbert calls "truthiness," a satirical term referring to something known on a gut level, without evidence. The concept has little sway in the rest of the world. Frey can't admit that he flat-out lied. He says he may not have told the facts as they were. But he *felt* them to be true. He didn't tell his facts to you; he felt his facties at you. They were truthy. And that was good enough for him. I was puzzled by the number of people who defended Frey. Clearly truthiness plays a big part in their own arrangements.

So I finally read Augusten Burroughs's *Running with Scissors*, years after it was published but just after the

Frey debacle. And for the first time, I couldn't bring myself to believe all of it. After some research, I now accept that his mother was a mad narcissist and that she and her possibly-autistic alcoholic husband gave Augusten up for adoption to their psychiatrist, a man who masturbated to pictures of Golda Meir and handed little Augusten over to the pedophile who lived in a barn in the backyard.

But I don't accept that the doctor used to predict the progress of the day according to his own excrement and that one of his teenage daughters would willingly extract the mortal coil from the toilet with a spatula and leave it on a picnic table out back to be dried by the sun. It may well have happened but I remain determinedly unconvinced.

First, call me picky but as an accomplished pastry chef, I don't think a spatula is up to the task. Perhaps one of those circular slotted spoons Chinese chefs use with their woks would be the lifter of choice. But even a fish slice wouldn't do the trick, depending of course on the doctor's output.

Second, teenage girls, accustomed to squalor as they are, have their limits and that would be one of them.

Third, the shrink who lived in a huge tumbledown house in a nice neighbourhood, a house that defined ramshackle, even he would drive the neighbours beyond any limit of tolerance if he built a human excrement art-installation on the picnic table in his back garden. It would be viewed, it would be smelled, it would attract flies and vermin.

Even if the spatula were the perfect kitchen tool, even if the girl, unlike U.S. Army torturers and the British diet hound and toilet inspector "Dr." Gillian McKeith, had overcome a universal human aversion, no neighbour would tolerate a poo festival out back.

I say this as a person who watches a neighbour take a specially saved plastic bread bag and a hand spade and monthly collect hundreds of tiny beige balls extruded by her yappy little dog. She saves it for the next garbage collection. I yearn to move to another city or petition City Hall for a new fence-height limit of 16 metres. I, dear Reader, am normal that way.

Also, I don't think anyone—and some of the people Augusten was growing up with who did this had enough remnants of sanity that they had jobs outside the home—would eat Kibbles as a snack. It's lumps of dried dog food that look like . . . well, there's a theme here and I'm not running with it.

Burroughs has rescued himself from a childhood so bad that you wish he had Asperger's Syndrome, as his brother does, because people with Asperger's have difficulty making emotional connections with others and are less likely to be hurt by living in a household of mental patients driven mad by a psychiatrist who is a dead ringer for Santa Claus. But there are things that don't seem possible.

This creeping doubt about misery memoirs has damaged the work of the great American humorist David Sedaris, who writes truthfully about his eccentric childhood, decades of dealing with nutcases while working in an apple-cannery, as a mover, a housecleaner, a performance artist and devoted drug user and alcoholic. People say Burroughs resembles Sedaris. But Sedaris is a kind, highly intelligent human being who, while strange, observes the strangeness of others with a keen awareness of his own peculiarities.

Burroughs is a book in himself, minus his upbringing, and it isn't amusing. It is tragic. "Not laughing," as my tiny stepdaughter used to say to me severely when I would tell a joke I thought would appeal to children, usually things that rhymed. (I was trying too hard and that never works with kids. They will not be courted.) All memoirs start to look dodgy to me in this light. When Gerald Durrell wrote *My Family and Other Animals,* the classic autobiography on "that rarest of things, a sunlit childhood" about his youth in Corfu, he made his brother, the late novelist Lawrence Durrell, a figure of idiocy. Indeed, he made everyone a figure of fun. What a collection of fumbling, foolish, well-meaning people.

And then we read about the suicide of Lawrence's daughter—he is said to have raped her—and the hopelessly sad, borderline criminal life of his other brother, and his sister's haphazard scary boardinghouse existence in post-war England, and Durrell's own pathetic end in a care home, soiling himself and left untended for days by family and friends who admired him but did not really love him. Durrell died like the animals he had put into zoos, surrounded by well-intentioned individuals.

The great British novelist and playwright John Mortimer was once accused by a reviewer of "covering pain with jokes." I asked him about this and he was taken

aback. Covering pain with jokes is the only possible attitude, he said, and he is of course right. Not everyone
manages it, but it is the stance to aim for.

Durrell never mentioned pain, but he was always
making jokes. Burroughs cannot be amusing, although he
can describe madness well, choosing just the right detail
to send the reader away heaving. But Sedaris is a comic
genius. He is Thurber, if not Wodehouse, and he is certainly Perelman. He has no "side," as the British say. He
thinks little of himself and I suspect accepts compliments with mystification.

The baddies have much to fear now. Before memoirs
became popular, child molesters had things very much
their own way, for instance. No more. Mary Tyler Moore
was a little girl when she was sexually assaulted by a
neighbour and her mother either didn't believe her or
didn't care. The British writer Jill Craigie was raped by
the historian Arthur Koestler, a revelation that caused
consternation at the university that was about to erect a
memorial to the man, plans hastily changing there. Alan
Bennett now writes of being cornered as a little boy by a
pedophile in a cinema. It is a terrifying story, but he typi-
cally insists on making little of it.

It does appear that a great many people—judging by
the stories we read of the prominent—were raped as children, and we have the Pain Memoir to credit for this
knowledge. Two—and as of last Friday, let's make that
three—of my closest friends now tell me of having been
sexually attacked by male family members when they
were children; another friend was raped by a psychopathic

dinner date, a professor, who put a pillow over her face. He was perfectly friendly afterwards, which was the terrifying thing, she said, aside from asphyxiation. They tell me this only because the Pain Memoir appeared in my lifetime and began to unwrap the real world for us, making it acceptable for us to tell our own stories.

And yet people still yearn for the mythical days when children were sent out to play. Nobody worried about molesters then. The truth is, the molesters didn't worry in those days either. They were home-free.

Children accept the lives they are given, which is one of the blessings of being a child. You're like an animal in that you don't question your own existence, you simply live it. But at some level, all children yearn for a "normal" family, knowing in their hearts that there is something very wrong: drunken parents, a central shared lie that is never articulated, a mystification about how Daddy brings in money, why Mummy sleeps all day, the relatives who are permanently shut out, the pills, the endless hasty moves.

Good memoirs are based on meticulous observation and no one is better at that than children. The interpretation of what the child saw comes later.

The odd thing is that there is nothing more fascinating than unperceptive people. In fact I know several people who are utterly incurious. They don't read. They watch a smattering of bad TV, though I'm guessing here, because they never talk about high and low culture or anything in between. They cannot catch a current reference beyond the year they turned twenty-one. If they're women, they have never worked and they despise women who do. They have never had any achievement or any ambition to achieve. Is it some sick element in me that is drawn to people like this? It mystifies my husband how I chat with them at parties or in stores. It's like talking to a parrot, whose best effort is to mouth your words back at you perfectly. But they don't know it. Tell me about your life, I urge them. They do say the most astonishing things, if only they knew it.

Sometimes I think the greatest loss of all is not the unexamined life (for Socrates was referring to examination of the self) but the unobserved life. Unobserved people are fascinating.

A woman named Sylvia Smith wrote a very strange little autobiography in 2001. She lived in London, had done various odd jobs throughout her life, had very little money, no education or sense of aesthetics, read nothing, took everything at face value, was plain. She sent in a manuscript and Canongate published it. It was called *Misadventures* and took the form of a series of vignettes. She would agree to meet a date at the station to have dinner at his house. Asked to bring sausages, she would. And he wouldn't show up. There she'd stand with her packet of tubular processed meats until she left alone to go home and fry them. That would be a chapter.

Or she would negotiate bath times with her fellow boarders and they would inevitably fall out. People cannot live together, I think. Smith had a habit of giving her age and the age of those she described at the start of every incident, as if she had been taught in grade school that this was a means of authentication. Instead, it sends out the hum of madness.

I swear, *Misadventures* was gripping stuff. What was distressing, though, was the newspaper feature writers who were sent out to interview Smith and failed to form any kind of connection with her or to translate her for their readers. She was not rich. She was not beautiful. She had never met the great and rarely the good. It was as if her kind were beyond the writers' ken. They dismissed her while nervously praising her publisher for having taken on such a nonentity, as though she were a member of another species.

But the fact is, she was normal. One thing I always remind myself when I walk about the streets of my own city is that I am the freak. I am endlessly thinking, rethinking, analyzing, watching, missing out on things that should claim my attention, my brain a buzzing mess. *I'm* the oddity.

A man named Joe Fiorito interviews normal people for my local paper. And I am sure his editor considers the column to be some kind of social service with a human face. The most startling interview he ever did was with a poverty-stricken Asian man who had been arrested for shoplifting at a drugstore. He had stolen skin-lightening cream. For he had noticed that brown-skinned people didn't make anything of themselves in this country. I hadn't even known such creams existed. I wanted to scream, Don't press charges. Give him a barrel of the stuff.

Ten years later, I was prescribed a birth control pill that my doctor explained had given me the "mask of pregnancy." There were slightly darker patches on my cheeks, something that pregnant women sometimes develop. She prescribed the same skin-lightening cream for my vanity that the man had stolen to survive. I wonder what happened to him.

Joe understands that the people he interviews are normal. He is the strange one, with his writing talent and his interest in cookery and his astonishing kindness. I am the weird one brooding over my tube of Lustral and what this means in the grand scheme of things, a tide of sorrow sloshing inside me.

This year, I read that there's an ingredient in the cream that may be carcinogenic. Is all of life like this, an accretion of odd facts that we hope will somehow form a pattern? Am I writing the book because my role is to figure out the pattern? I know I am worth less than I think. Writers are small people. They are on the fringe. They write their memoirs with great authority, not realizing that they're the minion of the group, the person who tells the story instead of just living it.

Better to write a memoir with humility, as Sedaris does. One of the great frustrations of the book world—and I suppose the journalism world, although it is a much more callous surface-skimming place—is that the right books don't sell. The bestseller lists contain books like *Minge: The Left Behind Code for Women Who Dish* that sustain publishers and yet you'd probably pay not to read them. Editors despair of trying to bring a great memoir to the attention of readers. Thanks to the book club, word of mouth, perhaps even Book Crossing, whose members leave books in public places for strangers to pick up, there's a wisp of hope. How else would good memoirs get a chance?

The best Second World War memoir (and like many people, I went through an intense Second World War phase) was *And No Birds Sang,* written by Farley Mowat, a Canadian writer of great reach. He could write comic novels, adventure novels for kids and scientific works, but at some point he sat down and wrote the tale of his joining the Hasty Pees, his father's army regiment, and fighting through Italy, including at the horrific battle for the citadel village of Assoro. The terror of Assoro was that it was a fortress on a mountain, perched on the edge of a massive cliff. The task was to climb the cliff in the dark, undetected by German sentries, and take the town.

Mowat is good at detail. His description of a German sniper slowly firing bullet after bullet at a donkey as it wiggled in agony until a disgusted Canadian soldier finished the animal off has stayed with me to this day. We are told that the Americans admire Canadian snipers in the latest war in Afghanistan. I think snipers are cowards. I despise them. How clever you are to shoot someone in the back.

Mowat describes a soldier falling forward at the waist, his body perfectly sliced in two by a series of bullets. Journalism doesn't tell you this; readers might disapprove of war if they knew such things happened.

Not until I read Robert Fisk's dispatches about Israel's war crimes against the Palestinians in *The Great War for Civilization: The Conquest of the Middle East* did I read war described in this way again. Fisk says that telling readers what is done to human bodies, especially those of civilians, is the key to reporting. We have no idea what war is. He tells us of a squishy feeling under his boots and the realization that he was standing on a pile of murdered civilians in a refugee camp, the pile gathered by Israeli bulldozers. He describes a halo of wooden clothes pegs around the head of a woman shot to death as she was hanging up her laundry. He describes the vomiting of reporters as they came upon the slaughter that was abetted by Ariel Sharon, a war criminal later elected leader of Israel (and now he's a vegetable, tra-la).

Thanks to those small details, I see the Sharonistas differently than many people do. Clothes pegs. Sharon's bulging face, the face of an assistant killer.

Henry James said writing was all about seeing the pattern in the carpet. It occurs to me that many modern readers won't get this. For one thing, everyone but me has fashionable planked wood flooring. Even if they have carpet, as I do, there's no pattern. My carpet is a flat expanse of grey. James was a Victorian, which means he lived in an era of such fantastically complicated patterned carpeting that staring at it would make you go mad like that woman in Charlotte Perkins Gilman's 1892 *The Yellow Wallpaper.* I love you, Henry, but the complexity of your novels goes beyond even the maddest of Victorian flooring.

Nevertheless, a Pain Memoir has to have some kind of pattern or theme. The Rotten Parents theme is probably the most fruitful, given that most parents are spectacularly inept—family values, indeed—even when they mean well. Subsets are Handed Over to Rotten Relatives (*City of One* by Francine Cournos, a great book by the way), Donated to Pedophile Cult (see Burroughs, above) and Evil Stepmother.

My favourite of this last subset is Helga Schneider's *Let Me Go*, if only because the author is a lovely person who to this day doesn't grasp that no court would convict her for having split her mother's head open with axe. Hers was a careerist mother. Helga's mother abandoned the family to join the SS and become a concentration camp guard who really loved her work and found the post-war years a letdown. Helga subsequently endured a sadistic stepmother (what are the odds?) and an orphanage.

Then as an adult, out of blasted hope, Helga takes her beautiful little son to meet the mother she has not seen since childhood. Mum ignores the child, fortunate boy, but makes a peace offering. She has handfuls of expensive jewellery, which Helga realizes instantly were stolen from Jewish and Romany women stripped as they entered the gas chamber. The reunion goes downhill from there, and later Helga visits her mother in a German old folks' home, where everyone knows she was a Nazi torturer partly because she still behaves like one. At this point, it's actually funny, because the staff and other patients show a saintly patience toward the hideously insane old woman who serves as a relic of an era for which Germans (and everyone else, I suppose) can't forgive themselves. It made me think better of Germans.

American Pain Memoir, Subset: Evil Mother writers aren't like Helga Schneider. They don't take any crap.

They take notes. An American writer would have smothered that woman with a pillow in 1967. Pain Memoirs, Subset: War, are often very fine, because the pattern in the carpet is of the individual as well as the mass. One of the greatest war memoirs is Roman Frister's *The Cap: The Price of a Life,* in which he explains the selfish human desire to survive, to the point of stealing a fellow prisoner's cap in Auschwitz to replace the one stolen by the *kapo* who has just sodomized him. The *kapo* has taken the cap of his latest victim, knowing that all prisoners without caps are automatically shot. The next morning, Frister watches the capless man shot to death at roll call.

Frister writes his memoir as he travels to a court where Wilhelm Kunde, the Nazi, is tried and sentenced. When he sees Kunde—the terrifying man who split the boy's beautiful mother's skull open with his pistol, in front of the child, her body falling to the polished wooden floor with a thud that Frister can still remember—he is numb and indifferent.

Kunde looks like a little old man in a suit too big for him, a tiny human doll. He is convicted and sentenced to seven years.

Frister thinks morality cannot be judged by one standard. It varies according to circumstance. He is right, but I notice that I have yet to meet anyone who has read Frister's great book. And that is the point of the memoir, to study uncomfortable questions like that, things otherwise left unsaid. Readers aren't happy with Frister's shrug, so to speak. Very few Second World War memoirs—and I swam in them for years, out of a moral

sense possibly, but more likely out of morbid fascination—
are like this, like a broken arm. Frister offers his jagged
limb; readers would prefer a nicely healed straight arm.

Thanks to the Americans, there are a great many war
memoirs, by soldiers, by little girls whose skin was
burned off by napalm from the Dow "Better Living
Through Chemicals" people, and by war photographers
like Don McCullin who can't shake their guilt.

There's a man named Andrew Neil who used to edit
fine papers bought by Rupert Murdoch and inevitably
bring them down to a low sour standard that would make
the good journalists who used to staff them weep. This
isn't necessarily to denigrate Neil, who stole the journal-
istic notion of "Treat light things seriously and serious
things lightly" from the *New Musical Express* staffed by
Julie Burchill et al., and made newspapers interesting
again. Worse, but interesting.

But I hate Andrew Neil because he fired McCullin,
one of the finest news photographers who ever lived.
McCullin's picture of a Biafran child, a boy, stooped over
with such a look of hurt in his eyes, sits in McCullin's own
Pain Memoir on a shelf behind me as I write this. I've
seen the picture twice, once as a child and once for the
purposes of this book. I suppose we'll call it Pain Memoir,
Subset: Photos of Misery. Neil's autobiography, on the
other hand, is fairly disposable. He's a dodgy man famous
for his deeply strange hair. I shan't recommend his book.

This brings us to Pain Memoir, Subset: I Am Deeply
Strange. These are written by people who travel the
foreign galaxies of suffering, always aware at some level

of the madness of their self-inflicted torture. Marya Hornbacher's bulimia memoir, *Wasted*, in which she neared death at 50 pounds and thus now knows she will die young, is informative. I do wonder, though, how a teenager who eats so much and vomits undigested food so frequently and lavishly that she repeatedly bursts the pipes of her parents' home . . . well, wouldn't anyone reading this book out of fellow feeling—a similar pipe-cracker—be beyond the help of literature?

Emily Colas's memoir of obsessive-compulsive disorder is a masterpiece. There isn't a word in it about the agony of existence, because Colas won't give herself the comfort. It's a comedy. A hideous comedy, true. Colas's misfortune was to marry a man who could cope with her fear that he might be putting cyanide in her food. As an enabler, he was excellent, but her description of the process they'd both go through so that she could safely brush her teeth takes three pages. It starts with the purchase of six toothbrushes and goes on to a packaging-leak test. Her title for the book? *Just Checking*.

As in the writing of David Sedaris, who had Tourette's and also OCD to an extraordinary degree but in later life managed to sublimate his jitters with cigarettes, even moving to Paris where he could smoke everywhere, anywhere, there's no analysis beyond an implied "Don't be like me. I was odder than fuck and it was unpleasant for those around me." Sedaris's mother, rather than putting him in hospital, made a joke of it. She took his condition as a given. This carpet has no pattern, Colas and Sedaris are saying, and I admire them for it.

The Pain Memoir, Subset: Abusive Husband, is huge. It's all entirely convincing and wrenching to read, but it has not made the police smarter or more determined to protect women and tiny children from the fists and knives of men. It may be the only Pain Memoir that has done no far-reaching good. Nevertheless, read them if your husband gets out of line. Keep a Running-Away Account at the bank. That's all I will say.

I don't really count Pain Memoir, Subset: Sexual Disorders, as real Pain Memoirs. Sex to me is a category in itself, partly because most good memoirs are written only after writers achieve a mastery over their material, a real understanding of what went wrong and precisely who was responsible. The pattern isn't in the carpet; it's painted on their reading glasses. And even the most sexually driven people cannot seem to successfully put into words why they'd go out looking to be gang-raped. The American writer Daphne Merkin is the only human who has ever explained why some people like to be spanked. One. Writer. Explains. That's a terrible success rate.

And frankly, no one's interested in why some people favour scatology. It's bad enough that they do, no one wants to wade through the incidents; there may be faint curiosity about what it tastes like but you're not going to pay for a book to find out. The materials are always close to hand if you wish to experiment. Only the childhood roots of the disorder are interesting. But no shit-fancier is ever clever enough to explain that one.

I must apologize, therefore, for the number of scatological references in this essay. Me, who won't even tolerate conversation on the subject, not even in daily life, and yet I dwell on it, as do Pain Memoirs. Kathryn Harrison wrote about her affair with her father, but what I remember of that book is her father's new wife pounding wheezing young Kathryn's back to free her lungs of mucus, even as she knew that Kathryn was sleeping with her husband/Kathryn's dad. She probably pounded hard.

Disgust plays a huge part in the Pain Memoir. People reveal their greatest hurts and shame. Sweat, shit, blood, all the excretions of the body stand for a greater pain. After all, we are tiny hairless animals. We don't look like much compared to the warriors of the animal kingdom. We are without beauty. Unclothed and bald, we understand, as animals do not, that we have been born and will inevitably die while suffering unspeakable hurts. This is why I don't find any subset of the Pain Memoir disgusting, although writing about scatology appalls me. The body isn't the problem. It's a manifestation of the mind and the mind is where the joy and the pain truly reside.

The Pain Memoir doesn't have a Mind subset. Mind is the essence of the genre. A memoir full of lies, as long as it is exposed, is actually an interesting subset. It should probably be classified within the I Am Deeply Strange subset.

There's a memoir inside you. Where would you put it?

You Can Check In Any Time You Like

*Unlike home, hotels are the real place where, when
you go there, they have to take you in*

 Hotels matter. Much
more than the revelations of the flight, or the uncertain-
ty of meals, or the traditional sights and the unexpected
horrors, or even the rituals of shopping that are as famil-
iar to me as eating, the hotel either shatters or makes
whole the holiday. This attitude was imprinted young. If
by accident you were ever lucky enough to spend a night
in a halfway decent hotel on one of those appalling
cross-country vacations-on-the-cheap you took with
your entire family while being carsick for 5,000 miles,

you too would have fallen in love with hotels and all their comforts.

Naturally, your idea of comfort is different if you are a hick child raised by eccentric Calvinists from Boonieville. Look, this is not a bad thing to be. Life ever after is always more interesting and pleasurable, at some level, than your childhood was.

Wow, the hotel has elevators. With buttons. *Dibs I get to press them,* every child sings out. (What is it with kids and buttons that light up and beep? Does nothing for me now. Most irritating modern sound: Trucks backing up. Beeping is a wise invention, no doubt, at the cost of annoying everyone who isn't about to be run over.)

A hotel has guests, all of them of interest to me. I come from a family that, as a matter of principle, didn't even hire babysitters. I shudder to think which principle that was. Was it that the sitters would meet us or we'd meet them? One of us would come out of it badly. So guests were fascinating to me, as were ice machines and coin-in-the-slot bed vibrators and shower curtains with chrome holes and rings, and the magic of clean linen and tidy rooms each afternoon. Hotels were heaven to me as soon as I stepped into my first one, and this has not changed, and never will.

I don't know if this is rare or not, but I take a picture of every hotel room I stay in (not when I'm working because that would be insane; work is work). I take a picture because I find art in the individuality of a bed. All beds are different. And I do it because it helps me to fall asleep; forever after, in the photo and in my mind, that bed will be there, even with God knows who sleeping in it, even as I lie sleepless in my bed at home. I wonder if you'll someday be able to Google Earth your hotel room bed.

The bed is always the centrepiece of the photo but the huge stack of purchased goods in brightly coloured paper shopping bags is a recurring theme. I will also photograph the bathroom if distinctive in any way. In France, this is not always the case, thanks to white tiling, so sometimes I photograph the bathroom to freeze my hardship in time. Ah, I vomited in the sink that night. Of course there was little left over after I had spewed used escargots over my husband's leg. He stood there helplessly holding what seemed a good idea at the time: a small bread plate. It was 3 a.m. It is always 3 a.m.

In Italy, the hotel room is always brown in many aspects. In France, the curtains look like a Hermes scarf. One must fight for *placards* (closets) and I cannot see how anyone other than a backpacker could live in a civilized manner with the tiny-wardrobe-in-the-corner rooms I have been shown. It's certainly possible to pave the entire room with open suitcases, but in France you drink, and therefore you stumble.

Which brings us to the mystery of travel to begin with. You have stuff at home, and you pack a selection of stuff to take on vacation and further sift stuff for whatever minor side trips you attempt, until you are left with what by definition must be the essentials of life. But the shoes are wrong and where is my makeup and take my word for it, go nowhere without a flannel nightie; at some point you will freeze your ass and wish you had packed it.

That's travel: deciding the essence of "stuff." It drives me mad, it really does. I have bags of little tubes and jars ready-packed and yet I have always forgotten something crucial. And yes, some things *are* crucial, crusty reader. I can see without a contact lens in my right eye but I gradually develop a crushing headache that is obviously related to the muscles holding my eyeball inside its casing. I can feel the eyeball pulling away. But I've forgotten my vision gear.

I forgot to pack the children's underwear in London once, which wouldn't have been so bad, but you try replacing it on Oxford Street on the hottest day of the year on what turns out to be Gay Pride Day and your hotel room isn't going to be ready until three. Jet lag chews at your sense of humour and the sheer grottiness of the city makes you feel as though you're in the middle of an Anita Brookner novel as it reaches its stunning climax. In other words, you feel odd and you need to lie down. The next twenty years will be a winding-down in a slightly depressed atmosphere. For some reason, your relatives will tolerate this. I don't understand Brookner heroines. If I did, I'd be mad in a foggy, genteel kind of way, right? *Incidents on the rue Laugier* was the worst. The protagonist spent decades unable to get off the couch after some guy failed to meet her at the tennis courts. And her husband put up with this nonsense. I must be making this up, but knowing the increasingly finely sieved novels of Brookner, I suspect I am not. Brookner wrote a novel

where the heroine, or the doormat as she would be iden-
tified in any other piece of fiction, had a sort of breakdown on a London street as she rushed to get home. (Was
it from a disastrous lunch at Durrants Hotel on George
Street? I've had that.) She had a terrible feeling of panic
and felt she could not release these feelings until she was
home but she could not find a taxi . . .

See, this is how I feel after a simple afternoon's
shopping in Holt Renfrew, a store I know by heart and
from which I obtain comfort. But there I'll be at Yonge
and Bloor in a complete state, a tizzy, longing to lie right
down on the sidewalk, almost as if someone had failed to
meet me at the tennis courts, but not quite that bad.
Brookner has that talent (obviously, since I remember
the scene) crucial to a novelist of making something out
of nothing.

And I have it as a *life* talent.

Hotel fanciers seize on all hotel references. In
another Brookner, I think they meet at the Basil Street
Hotel where I had the misfortune to stay once. It's the
kind of hotel that has little reading lamps with pale pink
shades all over the place, and where Joanna Trollope
does all her media interviews. In Robert Fisk's magiste-
rial history of the battle over the Middle East, he meets a
contact in the bar at the Hotel Lutetia in Paris. I stayed
there, I thought proudly as I read this. They were very
rude to me.

These are the thoughts one has on the hottest day of
the year on Oxford Street as one's children buy unnecessary bras at Marks & Spencer.

And then the hotel room is ready—it is three in the afternoon—and you hate the city that kept you awake for thirty-six hours of extra misery in a life that has had sufficient, thank you. You are in your room. You and your spouse unpack with great care. You wash and sleep. You are restored by this room that has been slept in by thousands of people who have left no mark.

I remember the hotel room next to us in Montreal being cleaned, and I do mean cleaned. Floorboards were being taken up. Walls were being sanded. It was the kind of cleaning that is necessary only after an expansive, bloody death. The Americans know this, having developed a sub-industry about a mile below Molly Maid based on the fact that most American deaths are messy thanks to their love of guns. Bone and brain tissue, flying, splattering organs, the smell that endures in the case of the long-dead and undiscovered. This kind of cleaning involves carpentry, and it's expensive. Hotels, like cruise ships, must get used to this.

The most luxurious hotel room I ever stayed in was at the then Regent in Hong Kong, right on the harbour. The water was a dark blue, although in Hong Kong you don't question things like that too closely, and turbulent. Everything in the bathroom(s) was marble. I hate marble, find it cold and ugly, as if someone in a temper has been scribbling on it. And the place was . . . watched. You'd press a button by accident and a white-jacketed room attendant would be at the door in twelve seconds, as if he'd been poised to pounce while watching through his spyglass. It bothered the hell out of me.

One of the attendants stank of sweat, which you do in Hong Kong, such effort does it take to make it through the streets at the best of times. But his was a fermented stink that came from days of not washing. I made myself smell it. Imagine how this young man lived, in a room perhaps, shared with six. How often did he have access to running water and the privacy to wash?

I had a hotel bathroom the size of his family apartment and a bed so big that I could roll over and over and not fall off. Smell his body smell, I told myself. That's how millions live in the square mile that surrounds you. That's the sham you have here in this city. That's why they struggle so, to rise above Fitzgerald's hot sweaty struggles of the poor.

There was one of those negative-edge pools on the roof of that hotel, the kind that gives you the illusion that you are sitting on the precipice of a waterfall, except this particular waterfall fell into Hong Kong's Victoria Harbour. It was the most fantastic, exciting, pleasurable place on earth to be, and I went there every day to wash the city off me. But I always had the feeling—I think it's intentional in Hong Kong and it will become intentional in all of China—that the point of the pool was not that I was revelling in this beautiful splashy glass teacup, but that others weren't.

If you feel this way in Hong Kong, where you are aware that everyone is capitalist to the back teeth and ready to smash ahead of you, imagine how you feel in Kolkata, where people have concerns besides capitalism and prove every day that they are not willing to smash ahead of you. Now that's shaming.

Since the extension of buying locally when you travel is that you try to return money to the people of the country you are visiting rather than to some multinational, I never stay in American hotels. In Kolkata we were at the Oberoi Grand, which is not just grand in comparison to what is outside the hotel gates—my toenail clippings were grand in comparison—but grand in itself.

Kolkata proved what I had always suspected: that I will not kill for food or glory but will for air conditioning. After the terrifying trip from the airport, throughout which I berated my husband nonstop about not having named a children's guardian ("and they're your children, you'd think you would have taken more care because we shall never see their faces again, our corpses probably won't even make it home, and I think they might well like to have your grave to visit; oh what a place to die, a flesh sandwich between two buses on a road with twelve lanes none of them marked or respected what hell have I ventured into I regret the life I have led oh I do" and on in that vein while the driver and his companion laughed at us), we arrived in the air-conditioned courtyard of the Oberoi where I restrained myself from kissing the marble (yes, marble) floor at check-in.

It only occurred to me later that we didn't need a guardian for my husband's children as they already had a mother, but as I say I was in a state.

My husband remembers the Oberoi fondly because he now lives with a level of insomnia that would trouble the magician in the water bubble, David Blaine. "We slept for eighteen hours on the bed in that room, eighteen solid hours," he says dreamily.

"Yes, and we were travelling for forty-eight," I say.

But it doesn't matter because it was the best, longest sleep he ever had. An outdoorsy type once explained to me why people love camping. You go without comfort so that when you get home, you see your perfectly ordinary house with new eyes and touch it with fingertips that tingle. Oh, the pleasure of a clean bathroom. You bounce your feet on the carpeting, the way I did when I visited my parents at Christmas during my poor student years. If I ever had any respect for tented people and their canoes, I lost it then when I heard this. It's all just deprivation by design?

But I understood better when I arrived at the Oberoi. And that time I'd only been in a perfectly nice plane for thirteen hours and a cab for one. I was screaming inside.

I never did get to the point where I could walk around the block where the Oberoi was situated without racing back to the room in tears. How can so many limbs go missing? What disease makes a person's face look as if it were melting? Indians are the most beautiful people on earth and it makes their suffering all the more painful to see.

In the end, I spent most of my time peering out the window at families living on an area of dirt and managing to keep meticulously clean by using water from a standpipe. People like me, us, our pleasures cause most of the global warming that will dry up the water in that standpipe—that would be my morning thought.

So I spent my time at the Oberoi very much *in* the Oberoi. It was an elegant, gracefully proportioned room (they use that phrase in decorating magazines but you don't recognize it until you see the genuine article) done in dark woods. It was so clean. I sent my khaki pants to the laundry and they came back beaten to death. They were sorry, those dirty trousers were, and I was sorry too because I knew the washing had been done by hand.

India is so crowded and so devoid of grass and empty pavement that dust gets everywhere. Every inch is filled. Thus Indians are fanatically clean. But an ad where a woman dances through the house for the sheer joy of Swiffering would bewilder them. Why does everything in the West have to be made into an orgasm? Cleaning is a duty, a necessity in a dirty world.

And by the way, Swiffering is not cleaning. Good. You already knew that.

The four-poster bed at the Oberoi is the bed I long to return to, despite the attendant anguish of its surroundings. Imagine you're in India, I think. Feel this clean white cloth that covers the bed that is soft but not too soft. See this dark wood. Smell this mysterious place. Watch the way the people measure their movements in the intense heat.

The city would black out but the lights would remain burning in the Oberoi, which had its own generator and its own clean water and would serve you toast and jam for supper if you couldn't cope with an onion bhaji.

I didn't know what to make of it all, but it did not seem to trouble anyone else. There were just my eyes staring out of my room's window, spying on the daily lives of the people who lived on the street. They would have thought a tent in Algonquin was *luxurium extremis*.

What does a hotel room need? A bed, chest of drawers, desk and chair, perhaps an armchair. Two bedside tables. Many lamps. And apparently a shower of such elaborate design that you are scalded or frozen but either way badly frightened. I always resent television, because television is the leveller that says you haven't left home. And the pornography astonishes me. I can sit in a hotel room in the Rocky Mountains and watch an increasingly dazed and pulpy woman have sex on a table with five hundred men. Can this be done? Apparently.

Lake Louise, named after one of the uglier ladies of the British royal family, winks at me like a lushly lashed turquoise eye. Everything looks sexual after the porno film *Houston 500*. My dinner is meaty, big and beaty. The fondue pot drips oozing diminishing chains of Gruyère. You think of mountain air as bracing, but that movie infects me with lassitude, as though the bones have melted in my body and I might slide off the chair like a Dali clock face.

Most odd. Who comes to the mountains for foreign pornography? Why would anyone volunteer for sex with five hundred men? What kind of men would immortalize themselves by agreeing to have themselves filmed attempting it? Why did I even ask that last question?

The days are gone now when I automatically enjoy all hotels. Sometimes I think this keen enjoyment of any-thing new, no matter how strange or awful it is, is the only thing I miss about youth. I once stayed at a Marriott beside the Mall of America in Bloomington, Minnesota, and thought I was having a wonderful time. I left my key card in the door slot, because that is the sort of thing I do when travelling alone—Mr. Bickerson isn't there to point it out—and the male attendant knocked on the door and slid the key under, warning me politely to be careful. Americans are so amazingly nice, I think. At least until they torture you by taking you to Camp Snoopy, the theme park inside the appalling place that is Mall of America. But I was in my thirties. Given my upbringing, I wasn't even clear who Snoopy was, or why adults would wish to visit a garish, deafening collection of kiddie rides even when they didn't have children to entertain. The obvious pedophile angle wasn't so big in those days (this was fifteen years ago).

I thought the mall was big, which is the way I liked my malls at the time, but even so, the stores were increasingly much of a muchness. The organ store was amusing, though. I took pictures of the salesman sitting alone in the store playing "Yellow Bird." I thought this was funny. I did not think it was the saddest thing on earth.

But then, I was thrilled to be staying in a Marriott.

Now, I'm the kind of person who shivers with disgust when she is sent by her publisher to a hotel where the coffee maker is kept in the bathroom. True, I have never seen this in any other hotel, so you'd think I'd just find it gross and interesting and go with that. Instead, I quiver, I retch.

Coffee? In the bathroom? I sound even to myself like Niles Crane, but I call the publicist and ask them if they could never book me into a Marriott again; find me a Canadian hotel, an old Canadian Pacific hotel, now known as Fairmont since they bought the American Fairmont chain. Two years later, the Fairmonts, including all the big Canadian railway station hotels, are sold to an Arab prince and an American speculator. No one raises an eyebrow.

I imagine we will all be making our coffee in the toilet now. This sounds too much like Harold Nicolson's remark to his wife Vita Sackville-West after the release of the post-war Berridge Report that aimed at bringing health and cleanliness to the 90 percent of Britons who weren't upper-class. I suppose we shall all shop at Woolworth's now, he said. For years I hated him for saying this.

Now I see his point. I suppose we shall all stay in Marriotts now, would be my version. Put me up against a wall and shoot me.

I'd like it to be in the courtyard of the Oberoi Grand, if you would grant me a last request. By the pool, please, with those lovely teak chaises longues with the backs that kept sliding slightly to the left until I collapsed on the tiles and had to be put aright by the attendant. Oh, how we laughed.

Because it was so funny, you see.

Specimen Day

Just fill the little bottle, please

 I suspect a great many people have stopped writing in their diaries since the re-election of Georgie in 2004. There's nothing happy to say. And it wasn't as if they insisted on recording only happy events back then; if they had, their diaries would be as smooth and empty as the freshly ironed Cuddledown fitted sheet I place on my bed every Friday morning. Like my diaries.

My diaries were never intended to record events anyway. Who wants to recall them in all their feckiness?

Reading them years later makes me wince. But I did use them to recall my state of mind, whatever I happened to be thinking about at the time. Like Virginia Woolf's diaries except seventeen thousand times less able and of no conceivable interest to any human in the future.

But I thought I should shove in a Specimen Day, by which I mean a day plucked at random, a sampling of whatever was irritating my epidermis. On June 20 of 2006, say.

Woke up feeling slightly better than usual. Since I mirror my husband's insomnia, I wake up three times a night, which would not be so bad, but really the last wake-up, hours before any sane person is conscious, is so 4:48 psychosis, thank you, playwright Sarah Kane, and I'm sorry you're dead although you were clearly determined to die, no one manages it with a shoelace while under suicide watch in a mental hospital unless they really really want to be done with it.

So I pop a pill, which my husband does not do because he believes it's the easy way out. He is British, therefore will take the hard way out, with Gravol, thus feeling dopey all the next day. Take a quarter of a Gravol for nausea, no more, I say. Gravol is a bad drug. All the worst drugs are over-the-counter. Why don't you go to the doctor, tell him you are going mad (or I am) from lack of sleep and get something that works for chrissakes, but he won't. He'd rather moan about it. So I have this trick now. He moans and I say, "That's awful, my love," and he feels comforted and I hear no more.

I do mean it, but I admit the "my love" is a bit formulaic at this point.

A welcome change in my life since I left my last job is
that I no longer wake up after this pre-dawn pill in the
throes of a bad dream. For sixteen years, I would dream of
being unable to escape a building.

This morning I awoke from a protracted dream in
which I was being given oral sex by some guy. This is a
euphemism, of course. The man had his entire head
inside my vagina and was working away obligingly
(although this is anatomically wrong of course) and it was
pleasurable. I could not reach orgasm so when he finally
took his head out after much dedicated work, he was pale,
wizened and wet, looking almost like a tadpole, a sea
creature. He'd done without oxygen and all that salty juice
had made him something of a SpongeBob, with human
eyes turning vaguely fishlike.

It was a change at least.

Stumble downstairs to read paper, ingest boxed
cereal poured into a bowl, shower, inspect garden, then
tackle the usual round of tasks that astound me as an
adult. They're mainly paperwork: tax instalments, bill
payments, forms to fill in, e-mails to answer or postpone
answering, a phone call to make to an editor who wants
me to write about the Photoshopping of the female face
on magazine covers (thus ensuring that we never look like
our pictures and thus never feel human), her unexpected
yes to a price per word that I'd hoped would repel her,
magazines to read out of duty, packages of books from
Waterstones, online shopping for Roman blinds so I don't
have to sew any more out of bloody white sailcloth for the
porch that bakes in the afternoon sun and fades the black

wicker furniture to white, $150 worth of Poudre T. LeClerc face powder to order from California because it is only available in person in Paris and I'm running out and you don't want to see my un-matted face . . .

What upsets me is the time and trouble it takes to grind through each task. I clearly remember not doing this sort of thing when I was young. And it isn't all to do with the fact that I rented an apartment then. Home ownership brings paperwork, but not this much. True, I didn't pay taxes then. I was poor. I didn't wear face powder either. My skin was young. I had no porch and little money to buy books, certainly none for magazines. I saw my friends or I wrote and phoned them. It was no hardship not to have e-mail.

I have spent hours on things that don't matter, although I know from the testimony of those who suffer from depression that the anguish of not doing these things far outweighs the boredom of doing them. They're like flea bites. Hundreds of flea bites.

Read Virginia Woolf's *Moments of Being,* her collection of essays read aloud to the Memoir Club set up in the forties or thereabouts by Molly McCarthy, married to the impossibly ill-focused and random-minded Desmond McCarthy. There is a coziness to this. Over the years I have tried to buy everything by and about Woolf worth purchasing, with the aim in mind that one day I shall retreat to my bed (or chaise longue. "*Vita brevis,* chaise longue," as my friend Joey says), read Woolf and occasionally dine on toast and jam and various hot drinks. Really, I would be perfectly content.

This may be the only link between my youth and these troubled years: I always wanted it to be just me and Virginia. Lord, how I want that Blair man to be gone so that we can plod around the south of England visiting all the houses Woolf did. A new book has just uncovered a series of holiday homes. Clearly they need me in the Home Counties. And I might even go to the much-deteriorated St. Ives in Cornwall again—the century has not been kind to that town—and try to see its good points. Point.

The computer man visits. After the last $800 bill, S. feels we are owed a free visit from Firesnacks, since the program that stores this book in complete safety has once again failed to function. Andrew attaches a lolling plug. The program springs into action. I urge him to send me a bill for driving to my home to straighten a plug.

Since the house is being eaten by squirrels, and they are squirrels of particular malevolence, I feel, I Google a firm that sells outdoor hardware gear type stuff and for $150 a "Transonic PRO Pest Repeller." It is intended to repel all animals from my garden, from mice to raccoons to deer. The noise it emits is apparently silent to humans, but deeply irritating to animals. Genius, I thought, I'll kill me some squirrels.

The black box arrives. After studying the chart on the back and the little icons that refer to the animals to be repelled, I realize that the sound the box emits to repel anything larger than a sow bug is deeply irritating to humans. It sounds like a giant woodchuck a thousand feet high clicking its teeth. I had been thinking more of a piercing sound, that ring tone they've developed that can be heard by teenagers but is inaudible to anyone over forty-five. I tested it on the Internet, and it was true. I couldn't hear this sound at 15,000 decibels.

What I have now is a device plugged into the mains on my deck that will repel earwigs from the area around my kitchen window. Anything else will laugh at my sound system, now turned down, which sound likes a tiny woman tapping the nail of her index finger on the bar as she waits for her date to arrive.

No, I won't take it back. I can't be arsed. At least my purchase has enabled me to keep the kitchen safe from earwigs. Not that I have ever been troubled by earwigs. But it won't be a problem to come.

Nighttime is a puzzle. Air conditioning? So wrong. Windows open? Yes. Fan? Not sure? Two blankets or one blanket? Can't decide. Have we PVRed Stewart and Colbert? Is the perimeter secured with the Protectron alarming device? Ground-floor windows closed? Lampe Berger sealed? Dehumidifier in basement emptied?

It is a specimen day, so unlike the specimen days of my youth which encompassed one or two things. It is not an improvement. Or is it an improvement? Discuss.

Meet the Brookstones

How to bankrupt yourself in solitary confinement

Ah, the new Brookstone catalogue is here and all is well. It makes me feel smart and superior, as well I should. For the Brookstone catalogue would lift the spirits of Polyfilla. I may be inert, I may harden and be painted over, says the spackle, but at least I don't sell $125 2-metre-long radio-controlled sharks that glide through the water, "bringing drama and excitement to your backyard pool."

"What's that?"

"It's a toy shark."

"What does it do?"

"It brings drama and excitement to my backyard pool."

That's the Brookstoner for you. They are a simple, hopeful people, hungry for novelty and easy to thrill, owners of mall-sized warehouses of crap gadgets that look good for four seconds until you think, Why? Or in the case of Red State Americans who are the Brookstone heartland clientele, Why not?

I have a history with Brookstone. I once ordered one of their gadgets over the phone, a Tranquil Moments sound machine for nighttime, and you can tell from how I write this how soothed I am today. It reached me months later and broke fairly promptly, but that wasn't the problem. It was the call from the bank that operates my credit card. A man on the other end sighed. "If you're Heather Mallick at your home number, you haven't just spent $12,000 in a New Jersey mall, have you."

No, I said. Please kill that card but good.

He did so, saying that someone had been given the number and had reproduced a false version of my card. The last purchase that had gone through was a Coach bag that I had actually yearned for but refused to buy as I was too poor in those days for Coach bags. That hurt. What shameless blowsy creature using my name was walking around New Jersey with something as understated and expensive as a Coach bag? The only possible link between me and New Jersey was my cross-border Brookstone transaction, so I phoned and told them that someone had hooked into our phone deal. I imagined this woman's vast call hall. I imagined the numbing of her brain that was necessary to deal with people who wanted to know if the pool shark was real. In a broad Southern accent, she told me that she had no idea what I was calling about and I should talk to her supervisor on Monday, and she said this in a voice that conveyed how little she cared about my credit card and New Jersey and twelve grand and the Coach bag snatched from my figurative Canadian hand, compared to her crap life.

Years after that, I am in a mall in San Diego, a city that is eerily soothing in its perfect weather and lack of anything to do. It's like a rest home for people who weren't much excited to begin with or a mental hospital the size of a city, with ocean breezes pleasant enough to calm you but yet not enough to flutter your cocktail napkin. It's as if they have set a Brookstone wind gadget to "puff." You try to find a decent restaurant or a good bookstore. There is none. You don't care. You order more wine. Time moves glacially in the way it did before we began hastily melting the glaciers. The waves come, the waves go.

A Brookstone representative in the mall offers to demonstrate a top-of-the-line back massager. It looks like a huge black padded electric hammer. That is what it feels like. He hits me on the back, thudding my flesh, my bones. I brace myself against a wall. He hits me again and again. I shout at him to stop, and turn and look at him with shock. Stop hitting me with a huge black padded electric hammer! It isn't normal. It isn't nice. This is a public space, not a motel room. I wander off, muttering. *Brookstone.*

A decade later, they're still trying to make a sale. That is so American. I admire that quality, being a person of no persistence myself. But then I goggle at the audacity, not the endless drive to sell, but the endless drive to sell *this*. Really, my mouth falls open and my eyeballs bulge. Who buys this stuff?

A third of Americans are obese and you just know Associated Press doesn't tell you how many are morbidly obese because it's too horrible and secretly shriekingly funny, even to Brookstone. Because Brookstone customers are either amazingly fat or they're headed that way. Something tells me they're Blue Staters growing into Red Staters, or Red Staters who have faced facts. Brookstone stuff is really expensive, even for madly stupid stuff.

Pools are very important to Brookstone. Most people *swim* in pools, you'd think, but in the Brookstone world view, pools are reasons for white people to float on massive loungers ("easily supports hundreds of pounds") accompanied by a Snack Buoy, a round red floating tray with five cup holders and a central compartment containing what appear to be thick slabs of Spam. The loungers also come with speakers in the headrest, controls on the armrest and an extra cup holder in the other armrest lest the Snack Buoy float out of reach. One lounger is motorized, with two handles and propellers under your ass. Another takes two people side by side, facing each other. "Now couples can enjoy a chat without straining their necks to talk." Yeah, I hate having to move my neck. My husband and I almost never bother to speak because of it.

The pool theme appears to have little to do with water. All the devices have one aim: to make even the smallest movement unnecessary. It seems odd, as you could just as easily do this (by this, I mean nothing) on the grass. At no point does Brookstone expect your body to touch water. A pool as a weight-gaining device. Interesting idea.

Next comes six pages of poolside hammocks for people who want that floaty sensation and the sight of water while having nothing to do with the nasty stuff. And you can buy gear like a personalized Coast Guard–approved lifeboat ring ("Griswold Family Pool") in case someone falls in by accident and has to be fished out and dried off. It doesn't say if it comes with a cup holder.

Then there's sporty stuff for people who play competitive group games, alone. There's a lone baseball containing an electronic device that measures the speed of your pitch, and a personal digital golf game with a little strip of AstroTurf and a screen that tells you all the stats for the shot you would have made had you been at an actual golf course losing some of that weight. This item cannot be shipped to California, Brookstone notes, but provides no explanation.

What? Yes, there is a drink caddy for golfers that shoots your prepared drink out of a dispenser disguised as an actual golf club. Fill with hot or cold beverages. They must be making this up.

This is how I measure everything: Would you sleep with someone who drank out of his golf club?

Next come exercise machines—treadmills, cardio steppers, exercise bikes and something called a Fold-A-

Way Elliptical Strider, which I think is a machine that makes you walk. To nowhere. I have a pure horror of pointless labour. To me, if you walk or ride a bike, you should get somewhere. So why not go outside instead of spending six hundred bucks to stay inside with the machine you're not going to use? Or burn some calories cleaning something. Cleaning's the sport for me.

My dislike of stationary exercise, especially if it doesn't even aid the power grid, comes from a passage in Margaret Drabble's novel *The Realms of Gold* (yes, I can find a literary reference for Brookstone. Did you think I couldn't?), where her citified heroine, long distant from her childhood rural life, is horrified to come upon a crowd of adults in a field "turning" stones. It unfolds that they are clearing the stones for a children's playground. Later, in a rural museum, she sees an eel stang used for "turning" eels. Of course, she misread it. It's for trapping eels.

Why would you turn an eel? And why would you build a pool whose water you won't touch and why not go for a walk instead of walking in place indoors to nowhere? It's the equivalent of harvesting rocks and spinning eels of an afternoon. But my objections would mystify the Brookstones, even stripped of the Drabble observations. It's gear, it's stuff, buy it, Brookstone urges.

Next comes comfort. Mattress pads, slippers, neck pillows, mattresses, and that most hideous thing, the massage chair. They cost about five grand. They look like giant black lumps in your living room, like Darth Vader in *Star Wars* if he sat down and you sat on him and his whole body quivered until you shook and shivered. It comes with a CD player in the headrest.

On the American sitcom *Frasier,* the sturdy and sensible Marty Crane once sat on one of these massage chairs that had Daphne and everyone else cooing. A horrified look appeared on Marty's face as he registered the sensation of the chair beneath him. "That's disgusting!" he shouted.

And it is, because it is suitable for someone who knows they will never again be embraced by another human being. You sit in the chair and the rollers hum up and down your back and your calves are squeezed and your feet rumbled and every part of your body is stroked and vibrated and quivered and oh it is wonderful wonderful and then you realize that your moaning has everyone in the high-end stereo shop staring at you with . . . understanding.

These are the socially acceptable black leather La-Z-Boy equivalents of blow-up sex dolls with skin that feels real and a vagina and anus that heat up. Call it what you like, Brookstone, but a massage chair is an admission of defeat. The whole catalogue is an homage to failure, but Brookstone doesn't care to see it that way. The stuff sells.

Then there's novelty sound gear, plus, for some reason, a lamp with a small silver Harley-Davidson motorcycle as a base. No ginger jars for Brookstone. The shade is imprinted with dozens of classic photos of unspecified classic . . . things. "The lamp also briefly revs its engine when turned on."

Then there's tooth-care stuff, but I don't care about teeth.

You can buy a device that measures your heart rate as you exercise, while tracking your speed and distance. The weird part is that it comes with a global positioning system device that tells you precisely where you are on the planet. But knowing the Brookstone customer, you're wearing this indoors on your treadmill, so this is just sad, if not scary. Brookstone's implying that you're trekking the Himalayan foothills but I suspect *someone's* still in their rec room watching a Rick Steves "Let's Go to Prague" travel show.

There are other devices. A turquoise Panasonic Epilator for instance. It plucks as it shaves as it holds skin down "with minimal pain," but if it mistook a bump for a hair, I can see things going badly wrong and my entire armpit being sucked into a hand-held. Hand-held what? the emergency room people will ask. I'm not sure, I'll say. They'll be pulling strips of skin out of the blades and trying to stick them back on my scarlet underarms. I think not.

The motion-activated soap dispenser would have pleased Howard Hughes in his later dementia but I see all kinds of problems for the sane. Sure, you don't have to pump your soap but you still have to turn taps off and on, use a towel and then a doorknob. Germs lurk. It's not a question of touching. They're in the air. Are you wearing your face mask? And what's the point if you're going to have sex?

It always comes back to sex. This whole catalogue is profoundly anti-sex. It doesn't make loneliness easier to bear, it actually enhances it, makes it more likely. It's a funny thing to pay for.

But here's a useful gadget. It was named the best overall key chain flashlight by *The Wall Street Journal*, Brookstone proudly announces. It has an LED bulb that will last 100,000 hours. Now, even the liveliest and most sociable of people will not spend 100,000 hours getting into their car and abode. That's 8,333 nights. That's twenty-three years. And why does Brookstone boast that it can be seen up to a mile away? This is a key chain for a mobster charged with body disposal. Who else would be out at night and in need of such a sturdy nonstop light source? On second thought, no, this is a tool for a serial killer.

I love the blood alcohol concentration device. You blow into it when you're drunk to see if you can drive. Then you drive. I think it just encourages people.

I don't love the tennis stand. It's a sort of tripod with a ball on a wire that plays tennis with you for hours and hours and helps you improve your swing. Tennis for people with no friends. So why is the next device a stainless-steel tub cooler that keeps thirty-two cans or five 2-litre bottles icy cold for twelve hours? You play tennis, run, float, sit, lounge, golf and sleep alone (Brookstone sells a special Tempur-Pedic body-shaped pillow that hugs you from head to crotch, just like a human would if it loved you) and now you're having a blowout party? With whom? I think it's a fantasy item to soothe the social aspirations of a Brookstoner, whose dreams will never be fulfilled unless you get out of the house and down your driveway, away from the Grill Alert Talking Remote Thermometer that tells you when your meat is cooked should you move three hundred feet away from the barbecue, the only reason for which would be to go to the bathroom because, God knows, you wouldn't have anyone there to chat to or you might strain your neck.

I'll end with the Motorized Grill Brush. You use it to clean your outdoor grill, thus possibly developing arm musculature that will attract the opposite sex, or any sex. But no, it's motorized. You don't have to tense a muscle, you saggy, lonely old Epilated hermit living in a Tucson subdivision and looking for love in the Brookstone catalogue.

Oh, you'll find love there. The creepy kind. Not the kind you dreamed of when you were young and taut, every skin cell awaiting the touch, the kiss, of the glorious friend-filled future you had planned. But you've got a chair that shivers. That's something. Thanks, Brookstone! Hit me again with your black leather hammer. Harder. Harder. Don't stop.

The Monstrous Regiment of Men

Psst, men are dull. That's why women are
always the target. We're interesting.

 The only thing to be said for the latest stream of books explaining why women are crap is that they're written by women. If a man ever wrote a book saying women killed feminism when they got jobs that paid better than other women's jobs, or women are all sluts starting from age nine, or women aren't as smart as men it's a scientific fact, or women are total cunts for thinking they can have it all when they can't have anything and I'll make sure of that. . . . well, that man would be dead now.

I think a British writer named Neil did say it once, possibly in a book or just an ill-considered magazine article, but all I remember is the newspaper article he wrote ten years later saying he never got another free-lance writing gig again, he was reduced to writing about stock car racing in Dagenham and his wife left him and took the kids and he had to pay her child support even though he never saw them and women had ruined his life because he said they were crap.

I felt sorry for him, while despising him for being such a whinger, but really, he should have just grovelled and let women peel his tongue and whittle away his typing fingers. The thing that really astounded me was that he had a girlfriend. She lived with him. There is nothing a man can do that will make him a total write-off to women. Even most serial killers have the love of a good woman.

It hardly seems fair. My father-in-law Harry fought in Burma and came home after the war to meet his son (my husband), conceived five years before, just before he sailed to the Far East. S. shook his father's hand at the train station and didn't like the strange man at all. Of course, S. wasn't my husband then, he was a five-year-old boy with a bad attitude. But Harry just got on with it, which is what people did then.

That is what we are told, but then you get those memoirs about fathers who spent their lives at the pub and came home every night to beat the family sense-less. They weren't getting on with it, were they? They were whingers.

And I don't like that in a man. No one does. It's not fair to men, but it's a fact. Men take up so much space in the world that whingeing takes them over that yellow line.

Don't worry, I also expend quite a bit of energy loathing and despising women who write books attacking women. But it's hard to work up a head of steam when the books keep coming and they're all patently written to make money by outraging other women. One tires. One has the sneaking feeling that the only reason women as a gender are constantly attacked is that only women are interesting enough to *invite* attack. Men are boring. They may run the world, and very badly too, but they do so in a dull way, without brio.

For example, *The Fog of War: Eleven Lessons from the Life of Robert S. McNamara*, that documentary in which he explains how he has been committing war crimes since he were a lad, is a fascinating film. He's just some geezer in a trench coat, but by virtue of having been born in the correct year and attending the right schools, he managed to burn one hundred thousand civilians to death in the Tokyo firestorm of the Second World War and then murder and poison millions of Vietnamese, Cambodians and Laotians in the sixties. McNamara then went on to ruin, oh, a billion lives with his mismanagement of the World Bank but the film doesn't even have time to get into that, nor the continuing effects of Agent Orange with children still being born pointy-headed and eyeless in Southeast Asia.

It's not even a conversation, it's a monologue, Me and My War Crimes, and they still can't fit everything in.

But here's the weird bit. McNamara himself is not an interesting man. Neither was Albert Speer. They had interesting jobs but nothing beyond that. This is common, this state of males as place-holders, digits that fill a space but don't advance things.

Men are boring. Women are interesting.

Women's lives are pretty miserable compared to men's, but we are simultaneously damnably interesting. If we were like men, you wouldn't be able to get thousands of books out of attacking us. They'd be accurate, dull books, and publishers don't go for those. There's no market. There is, however, a market for fanciful misogyny.

The odd thing is that even though I am alleged to be part of that market, and supposedly the kind of person who buys chick lit, or novels with "Girl" in the title and covers that match female genitals, i.e. all pink, I am almost male in the blankness of my understanding of the current male-female landscape and all that entails.

For I am married. I can never remember how long I have been married, partly because we were already living together when we got married and partly because I think marriage is inherently pointless. Love matters. I swear, it truly does. (Scurries off to do the math.) When you have been married for at least sixteen years and living together for longer than that, life inevitably has its low points. It's then that the question "How much do I love you?" is answered. And the answer—unspoken, naturally—is often "At this moment, very little indeed." (*Psst.* Don't ask. It's not a good time.)

My problem is that I love my husband more and more

with each passing year. And often I have these weird racing sensations when all the love intensifies like a sponge being squeezed and I find I love him more each passing day. He can also be profoundly annoying and a real clot about American movies. But we are at the point, particularly since he is seventeen years older than me, where we know we are going to be together until the end, like it or not. Sometimes we like it, sometimes not.

But 'tis done.

And so I haven't really understood anything anyone has said about men and women for decades. I am in love. Done and dusted. The idea of actually reading an article about "dating"—and what a cheap, nasty word that is—is abhorrent, much less writing one for pay.

I'm a child of the seventies. What's to say? You sleep with some guy and then you decide if you like him or not, I guess, is about as far as I would go with advice of a socio-sexual nature.

I'm not saying that I am good at being married, just that I am good at being a seventies person who doesn't really care either way. Two years after we went through an actual marriage ceremony (I wince at the photos. There's me in a purple Alfred Sung suit and a Bernie Taupin haircut caused by my hairdresser going into false labour just before we went to City Hall. *False* labour. I'm still bitter about that flat-top head), my husband sat me down and explained the rules of marriage to me.

I hadn't realized there were rules, but I listened, game to learn, as this man on his third marriage explained the deal to me. I'd been hauled to the altar because my two little stepdaughters seemed to think it was important that I become respectable. The youngest soon thereafter stopped referring to her father as "the man who sleeps beside you," so I assume it worked for her.

First, he said, both people have to agree upon any large financial expenditures. We were so broke. We weren't house-rich and cash-poor, we were house-poor and cash-poor. We had renovated his house partly to make it habitable for humans of hygiene and taste (my suggestion) and partly to give me the impression that I was not living in the house he had shared with his second wife, although I was. I thought that was weird. I wanted to buy a new house. We can do that, he said, brightly. We could buy a house without a driveway.

We live in an odd little neighbourhood built in a time when people got around without cars although I have no idea where they parked their horses. But I was so dumb that I hadn't realized that it was a big deal to have a drive-way where we lived, and the thought of fighting for park-ing near your house so you could bring the groceries in . . .

Look, my husband was playing on my naïveté and my familiarity with small towns. Where I grew up we had a three-car garage and parking for four more.

Anyway, we were sitting on the stairs and he was explaining to me that I couldn't buy a new blazer without consulting him. This struck me as unreal, especially since he had volunteered to pay his ex-wife's credit card bill for that Christmas because he thought that was fair to her. (And it *was* fair. This nice woman, mother of his children, wasn't having her best Christmas ever, was she?)

I didn't care about that, though. All I could hear was that I was going to spend the rest of my life asking some guy if I could buy garmentation. Anyway, I caved.

Eventually we had enough money that I didn't ask his advice on anything financial, not just because I didn't care to, but because I ran the finances. To this day, the man does not know how to get cash from a bank machine. He gets his cash from a special book where I put it for him. (It's called *The Oxford Book of Villains*, editor John Mortimer, and it's on his side of the bed where he can't miss it.) Recently I was bedridden and asked him to go to the bank to get a certified cheque for his daughter's school fees.

Our bank is the blue one, he said hesitantly.

It's unreal. Yes, it is indeed the blue one, I said, but it occurred to me that there was another bank that was a different shade of blue. This might confuse a financial innocent.

I have a brightly labelled set of files so that he can cope if I die suddenly (I no longer use the jocular phrase "hit by a bus" as I have a girlfriend whose sister was hit and killed by a bus as she walked her dog in the early morning light), but I've told him to go to the turquoise bank and ask a lady for help.

The second rule of marriage, he explained, is that you can't sleep with anyone else. I should state here that I didn't want to sleep with anyone else, but being a seventies person had just assumed that should the matter come up, it was fine. No, he said. You can't do that.

Never?

No, never.

I adjusted. But years into the marriage, I felt obliged to point out that I loved him so much that even if he slept with someone else I would still love him. Seventies people say things like this.

It then occurred to me that it wasn't wise to say this to a man. So I said that that would give me the same right. I would therefore sleep with the first man I saw, even though I didn't want to and it could be someone evil but I would still do it.

So things are quite simple for me, although according to TV shows like that show that now seems so elderly, *Sex and the City,* things are terribly complicated for everyone else. Women really do feel anguish at the idea of being single. I liked being single, I tell them. Then they have fits at the thought of not bearing children. Adopt, I say. Or find a guy with kids. That worked for me.

But women have a fixed idea of happiness and it makes them crazy. Perhaps men do too, but all they do is grunt when you ask them about it, and that's very very dull, isn't it?

Oh, you men are boring. Ask them how lunch went. Lunch with a friend. Fine, they say. Ask them about their first wives. Can't remember, they answer. Why did you have children? Dunno. Why does it take you three years to not put up trellis on the garden shed, by which time I have hired someone to do it, and then another three years to fail to take it down? The time wasn't right, they say.

But ask my husband why *Ulverton,* which I know to be one of the greatest novels of English life ever written, is in his opinion total bollocks and you can't shut him up.

Etymology's all wrong for starters . . . and it goes from there, and it doesn't matter when I say that the *London Review of Books* didn't say that and they're mad for punctilious etymology, because they are wrong and he is right. He thinks German racer Michael Schumacher should be charged with attempted murder ("That's not aggressive driving, that's homicide") and neocons were just boys who couldn't do sports at school, but ask him why—not if, but why—he loves me and he has nothing to say.

Do you have any faults? I ask. I could discourse for days on my faults. He thinks for a moment, just to be tactful I suspect, but has no answer. George W. Bush had no answer either, I say. No, he was asked if he had made any mistakes in the first part of his administration. That's different. Okay, but do you have any faults? He shrugs.

He has never had anything to say about work, because he doesn't see other people as objects of contemplation. It's just work. Whereas for a woman, the workplace is a cauldron of pus and tears, and I could speak on it forever.

My husband is the only man I've ever met who is cleverer than me. And yet, like all men, he sees life as a simple thing. I see choppy seas, he sees a calm sail.

This is boring. I'm sorry but it is.

I don't even understand how men can write novels. They don't write them well, do they, even if their novels get the attention and women have to set up an Orange Prize just to win something. Male novelists, when you meet them, are often quite dull, and you realize that any fire they had all went into the making of the book. There's nothing left over.

My women friends, on the other hand, are fascinating. My aesthetician is fascinating. Witchy music comes out of the speakers in a darkened room as I lie naked and she spreads seaweed paste on my face. But that's not the neat part. It's the stories she tells. Everything is of interest to her. She can see that climate change is happening, she says, because the increase in officially measured Bad Air Days corresponds to the fact that the material taken from her clients' facial microdermabrasions is darker now. That's practically a news story.

My stepdaughters bought their father a facial and a pedicure for his birthday. He has yet to use the gift card. Why? I say. Actually I say, Why why why why why, for God's sake why not just use the fucking thing just go and get your hooves scraped why not why not why not? And he doesn't know why not but it's like the trellis on the shed. The time isn't right.

I hate to use my husband as an example but I want to show that a man can have the finest mind extant and be the best and bravest person I will ever know and yet here's the difference. I can meet a female politician and form instant common ground with her by asking if her husband understands the concept of a kitchen sink plug. She shrieks and says, You know, he'll see the sink plug filled with little bits of stuff and then he'll turn it over and empty it into the sink. And I say, Why do we have it if you're not going to put the stuff in the garbage? And I say, Does he rearrange your dish placement in the dishwasher too? And we're off.

I see men as monoliths, some kind of simple mute oblong thing. Whereas women are a light show, the northern lights flashing wildly all over the night sky. They can't be painted, can't be pinned down. The director Joseph Mankiewicz, who made *All About Eve*, said men, in comparison with women, were as complicated as alphabet blocks.

When women are vicious—and they frequently are vicious because they haven't the power to display their frustration in other ways—they are brilliant. I could get a book out of the women who have hated me or whom I have hated and translate each snarky remark, each stab of the knife at my spine and the squiggly, wriggling, shooting trail that led to a confrontation. With several exceptions, and those women were psychotic and posed an actual danger to me, I regret every friendship I ever lost because I think now that we could have sat down and talked honestly and worked it out. My own habit of cruelty is clear to me and it is shameful. When I feel wronged, I cut people off. I don't just hack at the rope, the way mountain climber Simon Yates did for sane reasons in *Touching the Void* but I break base camp and go home. The dumped friend shows up frostbitten and with a broken, gangrenous leg to find no tents, just a sewage hole and a blackened firepit. I don't admire this in myself. It's unfeminist and, worse, it's morally indecent. I suppose I just can't be bothered rebuilding a friendship with a man as it's a sandcastle anyway, merely temporary. But I never think I can undo the Gordian knot that a quarrel between females becomes. These knots can come into being without a word being said.

Don't underrate us, S. says. Men hate men too. They can be grubby and venomous in a way that is traditionally defined and despised as feminine. Entire companies pay the price because the boss is a malevolent dwarf and keenly aware of it. He'll take revenge for every inch he doesn't have, because other men will mock his height (women are indifferent to height).

As for women, men get very angry at the possibility that women are smarter than them, S. says, but it goes much deeper than this. He says men are terrified of the sexual insatiability of women. They know they can never satisfy it and they resent and fear this. This explains the extraordinary sadism they display toward even the women they meet in everyday life.

I suspect he's right. But I wonder if men don't also deeply resent how complicated and infinitely interesting women tend to be. They know that we're the dish rack and they're the flat rubber mat that goes underneath, so dull that there isn't even a name for it. They're just the flat-rubber-mat-that-goes-underneath.

It's oblong, useful, simple and mute.

Perhaps I shall never write again, having written this. But then, men don't buy the books, do they? Heh heh.

Give Me Taxes

And death doesn't upset me, by the way

 What's a sure thing? My husband's love is a sure thing. Or is it? How unfashionable to suggest that it might be. But if not, we're left with crotchety, big-bellied Benjamin Franklin's doubtless gout-inspired "death and taxes." He was wrong.

Death is a hateful dragnet, except when it's a blessed release, a tidy designer Seconal death surrounded by those you love (notice how I didn't insert the standard "family" there? I will never candy-coat things for you). I always think of the lotus-eaters in *Ulysses*. You can get high reading Tennyson's rendition of them. Death, mmm. Even auto-erotic asphyxiation sounds bloody good, as long as you don't realize toward the end of the best orgasm you ever had that you've gone too far this time and your funeral is going to be hugely embarrassing for people who actually liked you and a hoot for people who didn't.

But taxes are great. (Darling editor, what follows isn't entirely new, I've been saying it for decades; but it's my book.) I may be alone in this opinion but hear me out, please. I'm a fan of civilization, and taxes enable civilization. To put it another way, taxes grease the skids of living well.

Other people say loudly, endlessly, tediously that they hate taxes. They haven't considered the alternative, so let's embarrass them by doing that. They'd prefer to live in sod houses and spend their days combining a drop of oxygen and two drops of hydrogen so they can have homemade water rather than have it piped to their homes by tax-supported civilization. Fine, if it keeps them occupied and far away from me.

But I do not like to see civilized Canadians falling for sodbuster notions.

Right-wing people have many obsessions but their main one is taxes.

(This is a shame; wouldn't it be splendid if they were obsessed, simply single-mindedly blind, about something useful like clean water for the planet? Or making sure no one could graduate from high school without having read all of Shakespeare, and that includes memorization?

Think how much higher would be the level of abuse they could then level at the rest of us. I dream.)

They think taxes should be cut to absolutely minimal levels, if that. I don't know why free Canadian health care for all bothers them so much. You pay your medical fees in taxes or you owe them (yeah, sue me) to some lousy cheese-paring corporation that doesn't care about your privacy or indeed the success of your operation and the smooth running of your spleen, whatever that is. You pay your doctor one way or another; why get hung up with the name you write on the cheque?

To them, taxes are tapeworms, "bubble bubble toil and taxes," as Shakespeare's witches didn't put it, stealing all that is good. If you didn't pay Canadian taxes, you could have Porthault sheets instead of Yves Delorme is the neocon message to the rich. Without taxes, the middle classes could have Frette sheets instead of Martex. Without taxes, the working poor could have sheets. Without taxes, the poor could have a mattress on the floor and the homeless could have nicer cardboard.

This is absurd.

I pay taxes. I love taxes. When you work, the government yanks it off your paycheque. When you write, as I do, you take your receipts to Joan, my accountant, and give her a blank cheque made out to the Receiver General. The government uses it to do all the stuff you'd rather not think about.

Tax. A short word, an abused little shrimp-shaped thing, brutally misunderstood (as Lynne Truss, punctuation queen, says of the apostrophe). Yet truly the word *tax* trails clouds of glory.

When I was a child, I assumed the world, including my body, was run by tiny people in uniform. They carried electricity in buckets to feed the light bulbs, lit invisible campfires inside the oven and pushed at my hair from inside my head to make it grow.

Later, I learned this was nonsense. There were no elves cycling madly inside the car engine. (Ironically, after globalization, this was no longer nonsense. Little people did indeed beaver away in sweatshops worldwide to make my jeans and toothbrushes.)

Taxes ease our daily lives in ways we take for granted. They pay for new combed-concrete sidewalks, traffic lights, sewers, garbage pickup, nicely dressed diplomats so we don't show up at the G8 in golf shorts, ferries, fish in general, nuclear power plant inspection, protecting the provincial flower ("Leave that wild rose alone, ma'am"), libraries, white-coated people who spring into action when you contract flesh-eating disease, building codes, schools, dangerous-toy advisories, keeping cable companies in line, clean air, truck inspections for airborne wheels, loan forgiveness, autopsies, massage therapy, campgrounds, divorce, licence plates so you can track the guy on the cell phone in his Humvee who hit you, fluoridation, teacher training, privacy, universities, fair elections, fire trucks, child guardianship, hazardous waste control, name changes, hostels, museums, protocol (see golf shorts), trees, zoning, high-tech passports, standards in general, notary publics, noise control, organ donation, human rights, disability, drainage, bingo permits, boating safety, French language services, neighbour encroachment, aboriginal business aid, art galleries, adoption, jury duty, cemeteries, soil quality, spills response, tattoo parlour inspection, bank deposit insurance, street lighting, commercial ship registry, victim assistance ("there, there"), SINs, joint rescue (water and air, nothing to do with knees), aerial mapping, pesticide disapproval, and savings bonds.

Without taxes, you'd have to do all of the above yourself. Sure, you can contract it to the private sector, but if you've ever watched *The Sopranos,* you know the mob isn't actually any good at garbage collection. Landfill is just a means of corpse disposal.

Fine, cut my taxes and I'll pick a task. I'll take "spills response" and use recycled paper towels. Oh, you say the spill covers 2,000 hectares and it's sticky, oily and toxic? I thought we were talking coffee. Somebody call the feds. I'm a taxpayer!

Here in Canada, we believe in the public good, as in "good for all the public." (I'm quietly humming, *"He ain't heavy, he's my brother"* as you read this.) We don't believe in private affluence and public squalor. We like to balance those two things. Whenever you get upset by taxation, think of an ill-considered purchase. Then figure out what that cash could have contributed to, had it been in government hands. A gleaming new hip for your mother? Quality CBC television? An ice rink for kids on the reserve?

Paying taxes is a means to a good end. Can we do it with a lighter heart, please?

Such is the obsession with lowering taxes that all kinds of things are becoming less pleasant. Toronto, desperate for money, began setting up what I call garbage cans and what they call "landfill sorting centres" on the sidewalk, massive things with ads on the side, yer garbage can that pays its way. And I couldn't see what the fuss was about because I was looking at the smaller three-way bins with holes for different kinds of garbage (a decision everyone will get wrong anyway).

Then I saw one of these "centres," a gleaming condo tower on the sidewalk, and realized why people were so upset. They're *huge*. You can't see past the garbage condo to safely make a right turn. And especially given the advertising girth of these things, the pickup people haven't got it quite right. Someone has to *empty* them occasionally. If not, pedestrians will stuff diapers, coffee cups and newspapers into the glass-bottles slot, or the plastics slot, whatever they can find. When the pullout slots overflow, they'll throw apple cores on top of the tower and surround the thing with dodgy-looking wads of stuff.

You'd think this would drive skewers into obsessive-compulsives like me, but I look at it as evidence of human sweetness. Yes, they got it wrong, but only because the city got it wrong by not emptying the thing. So people aimed their discards vaguely in the direction of the gleaming, advertising-poster-plastered landfill disposal centre and hoped for the best. I suspect in low-tax U.S. cities they just knock the Tower O'Slop over for the sheer fun of it and hump it while on crystal meth, leaving the recycling slots empty even of inappropriate garbage but the bin covered in semen and dribble and, inevitably, blood. I kind of admire this. Americans get rambunctious. They don't use their words.

When I were a lad, there were bins and you put things in them. I know I sound as if I'm 102 but garbage didn't register when I was young because the government in some form picked the junk up.

Oh, those were good times. Naturally, we didn't know that because they weren't good times at all, but what I'm saying is that tax-wise, life was fine. There was a logic to things and somehow it was arranged that you did right without having to think about it. You didn't litter. In return, the bins were emptied. By taxes.

You take my meaning.

What interests me is that I sound like an old fool. I know my publisher would like me to sound young and hip, and yes, I am in some ways—I wear L.A.M.B. clothes by Gwen Stefani—but I don't sound as though I am. I sound creaky.

What garbage slot is designed for me? Neither plastic, nor glass, nor paper I be. God, I remember someone introducing the magnificent Doris Lessing at some godawful luncheon thing where they toast the Queen— how did I get roped into this? she must have thought, fondling a cruet—and they described her mind as a compost heap, out of which great things emerged.

Compost, that's me. And if something vaguely interesting comes out of the steaming heap that is my brain, then it's all to the good. Now I shall pour a glass of Côtes-du-Rhône and raise it to the greatness of our taxation. *Santé!*

After the Love Is Gone

Or why Britain sucks

 Other people have crushes on people. Me, I have crushes on countries. It's quite convenient in the sense that you can visit them and then you can leave without hurting their feelings. This is notoriously difficult to do with people you are sleeping with, as someone always blows hot as the other blows cold, emotions grow like blossoms and then like roots, and suddenly a visit isn't just a visit, it's a map of the future.

I haven't been back to Britain since the late nineties. A Brit on a talk-thread called "I'm watching *Friends*

on ecstasy while checking my soaring dot-com share values . . . yeah it's sooo 1990s" writes that he remembers watching "Ken and Barbara Follett attempt to open a giant bottle of champagne at Labour HQ on the night of the 1997 election, but fail. A little voice inside me wondered whether this was an omen."

It was. I'm not going back until Tony Blair's gone, and I may not go back until I forgive Britons for not having turfed him out once they discovered that he was a liar, a sociopath, a snaggle-toothed, meretricious, Uriah Heepish wide-boy, a disgrace to the European Community and an embarrassment to the nation that bred him.

But you can love a country while hating it. And I have to admit I still love Britain by deed, if not by my physical presence.

I was raised to love the place. Look at the ur-British books I read as a child: all the Swallows and Amazons sailing books by Arthur Ransome, Enid Blyton, *The Little Princess* by Frances Hodgson Burnett, historical children's fiction by Henry Treece, Rosemary Sutcliffe and Cynthia Harnett, books about otters, whales and foxes, about picnics and cups of cocoa and hard-boiled eggs under a sunny sky with jolly people.

The essence of British children's books is that Brits take their pleasures small. I cannot say how modern British children cope with the idea of a jam sandwich being the highlight of a day at the beach, particularly when they encounter an actual British beach that doesn't have sand but pebbles. And you need windbreaks, little fabric fences you put up in front of your family plot of pebbles to shelter you from the biting wind. And then there's the outflow of untreated sewage that made the EU declare most of Britain's beaches out of bounds. Britain retaliated by declassifying the beaches as actual beaches. They came out with another name, something like "wet edges" presumably, and got around the regulations that way.

It's all very well for a child like me to have enjoyed reading about small pleasures, as I had no pleasures whatsoever when I was growing up. But your modern North American child, his home choked with brightly coloured plastic items and expensive electronic gear that ups the ante each Christmas? I don't see the appeal for him in reading about the joys of jam sandwiches.

But I was hooked. As a teenager, I read mostly American crap as that was what was available, but my university years studying English Lit clinched the deal. I was in love with English writing, which is playful, elaborate, varied, elegant, all those good things. (American writing, which crested in the nineteenth and early twentieth century, had turned pretentious and dull.) I imagined words as an ocean. You could just plunge into it and do what you will.

British newspapers were still good then. Now, when even broadsheets resemble tabloids in their effort to reach the lower orders—I do mean this and it has nothing to do with wealth or education, only intelligence—the British papers far outdo the rest of the world in brave reporting and wonderful presentation. For that's the thing. Brits are interesting.

And I was mainlining Virginia Woolf. I came in at the beginning of the Bloomsbury craze when I studied her at university and realized that the book I had greatly enjoyed, *The Waves*, was not the book Woolf had actually written. The woman needed some explaining. And I was off.

Once you are enamoured of writers you explore their milieu, which I began to do on my honeymoon. My husband was British-born, although he had left the place with some disgust decades before. It's a peasant country, he warned me. And it is. But I didn't see that then. It wasn't so apparent as it is now.

I repeatedly travelled to London, always with an elation I have rarely equalled since then. To me, London is a network of blue plaques where writers lived and it is a festival of good shopping. Thanks to the immigration that whitish Brits decry, it is possible to eat wonderful food there. I stayed in good hotels, not great ones. There are no great hotels in the British Isles. It isn't the nature of the place.

I visited Virginia's house, Monks House in Rodmell, Sussex, her homes in Bloomsbury, and all the good places, like Kew and the National Portrait Gallery, the Tates and all the places fashionable Brits decry, mainly because they talk and write so much and there aren't enough opinions to go around.

But the best of London isn't Britain. It isn't even London. Britain is a shit-hole. Venture outside London and you will find a poisonous self-destructive place filled with pig-ignorant people that elect governments that do maximum damage. Thatcher began privatization but Blair continued it. Imagine privatizing water. Britain did this. With global warming, there is an annual hosepipe ban now in a country that regularly suffers from massive flooding. Water bills are fantastically high, but the water itself leaks away through crumbling pipes that haven't been upgraded for centuries. It is not in the interest of a private company to spend its profits on replacing ancient pipes. Why should they? They find water shortages helpful. It's not as though we're trying to find a replacement for water the way we are for fossil fuels. Water's rarity is a precious thing to a corporation without any concept of the public good.

What kind of country spends £1 billion planning the privatization of the postal service, renames the Royal Mail "Consignia" and then gives up, realizing that the mail will go the way of water and railways? It will be a mess.

I did try to look on the bright side of a country that increasingly frightened me. No one does squalor better than the Brits. You can go into a Little Chef off one of Britain's endless pointless motorways, look at a menu so lurid it looks like you're being handed stills from an operation on your filtration organs—spleen, liver, et cetera—and then you can eat something that is clearly not food. It is matter, greasy matter.

And then you can drive to St. Ives, where the young Virginia took family holidays for about fourteen years until the death of her mother. She lived at Talland House, a beautiful home now surrounded by cheap, crappy, badly designed modern buildings and torn apart to make flats for people who've never heard of Woolf. Any other country would turn Talland House into a shrine. All I remember is a morbidly obese man wearing a stained wife-beater with skin burned the colour of a hothouse tomato standing in a giant parking lot outside the house. He had just bought the place. Everyone in St. Ives looked like him. For this is your British tourist. People complain about fat, loud Americans but the Brit peasant has them beat on sight alone.

I was in a bad mood, having cut myself badly on the harsh toilet paper at the St. Ives public toilets—I know this sounds impossible but believe me, it is not—and I was limping and hoping no actual blood was flowing. We went down to the seashore where the sand was the colour of cream and the sea was the freshest, most beautiful warmed turquoise I had ever seen. Godrevy Lighthouse stood in the distance as it had in Virginia's time. Stand on the shore and look out. England is very fine indeed. But behind me was a municipal festival of dog droppings and shops selling horrible candy and frying mystery meat at grotesque prices.

I have never been so disappointed, so angry. Cornwall had a beautiful town with a distinguished history built on a hillside facing out to a seascape that would make Turner faint and they turned it into a dirty, raucous, crowded place with broken pavements and shambling hovels that smelled of deep-fat fryers and hairy armpits.

There were poor people in Virginia's time. Her mother, already nearing an early death, used to exhaust herself caring for the poor of St. Ives. But photographs don't show this kind of public self-destruction. I think there were small pleasures then, even for the poor. There are no pleasures, large or small, in St. Ives now, beyond the ones Nature gave to the seashore.

St. Ives is emblematic. For Britain was always a peasant country with a gap between rich and poor that rivalled what the Americans are creating today. The Second World War finished Britain off. The architects of the sixties did murder most foul with their great heaps of concrete, a material that stains in the rain in that rainy country, and then the postmodernists came along. Instead of repairing the remains of the beautiful architecture that once graced the place, they build glass gherkins. It's not a country suited to glass or to fibreglass Georgian columns—the Turkey Twizzlers of architecture, says Alain de Botton. It's suited to the vernacular stone, to brickwork, to symmetry.

There are wonderful dreamers like Thomas Heatherwick building a plaza like a just-unrolled carpet of blue glass in the middle of Newcastle. It is made out of old bottles; Newcastle is an alcoholic's paradise. But there are so few of these designers.

The great thing about Britain has always been its eccentrics, which is not the right word. They are people who fizz with personality, who are interesting in themselves and don't give a toss what other people think of them. Eddie Izzard, one of the greatest stand-up comics, started out by busking with comedy routines in Covent Garden. He was told he was crap, he said. Most people would slink away. His crapness was what sustained him, he said. And he wanted to be a heterosexual transvestite, so he did that.

Britain even has great politicians. I don't mean the Manny Shinwells, Tony Benns, Barbara Castles and the Gerald Kaufmans who honour our species, I mean

the MPs with actual personalities, like the fuckable mess
Boris Johnson and the constantly fucked Alan Clark, who
wrote his great confessional (actually brayingly boastful)
diaries, and George Galloway and the magnificent back-
benchers who say fuck you to Blair and suffer for it with
honour. But they're so few in number.

Five percent of the population is intelligent (in
Britain that means fucking brilliant as in Great Fucking
Brilliant Britain) and most of the population is funny.
Brits are outrageous; they make me howl. The place is full
of Izzards; it's the only thing that makes the country
worthwhile.

The government is composed of lying bastards. It's
hard to pick the lowest point in British politics. But I took
it to be the suicide of Dr. David Kelly, a distinguished
decent man who told a BBC reporter that the government
was lying about the "evidence" that would justify its invasion of Iraq. Kelly was publicly hanged, drawn and quar-
tered by his employers. Within days, he quietly went for
an evening walk and slit his wrists under a tree. He lay
there through the night, eventually bleeding to death.

The Hutton Report was engineered to exonerate the
government of any wrongdoing in the matter. The prime
minister's wife, the peculiar Cherie Blair, and her husband's brutal hatchetman Alastair Campbell, signed a
copy of the report and auctioned it off several years later.
They could not have been more cruel had they signed it in
David Kelly's blood.

But the Blair years were full of moral monstrosities
like that. One prominent Briton said he had gone off Blair

(remember, Blair was elected as an honest Labour prime minister who would undo the economic brutality of the Thatcher years) when he read from the Bible at Princess Diana's funeral. The reading was full of unnatural pauses, all wrongly placed and hideously staged. It's painful to listen to, so phony it is. And this man realized that Blair was acting. It was only the badness of his acting that made it apparent. But everything was done for show, for spin. Truthfulness had vanished. It was laughable, no longer a virtue.

And I began to hate Britain.

It's ironic that my hatred of Britain coincided with a noticeable slide in the quality of British literature. But I may be wrong. Perhaps it has always been this way. Only a fraction of what was published was any good. It used to be you'd find some nugget in almost anything. But generally publishers were putting profit over quality, just as politicians were putting spin over actual good results.

Everything was turning to crap. It left a great gulf in my life, as I dropped one newspaper after another and essentially abandoned the reading of current fiction. There are always enough classics to occupy me, but when Michael Frayn, Doris Lessing and Margaret Drabble die . . . That generation is dying out, and there are few wonderful young writers to replace them. I no longer see the point of fiction at all if it is going to be done this badly, but it was only when the rot began in Britain that I realized this.

Britain is so grotty. They don't even do those quiet ingenious little murders now where the neighbours only find out when there's a funny smell from the drains. It's drive-by shootings and thugs torturing the other thugs on the housing estates because Blair won't spend money on the poor and there's no other way to pass the time. Unemployment is massive on the north side of the divide. Schools are whirlpools of failure. People get fatter and sadder and angrier every hour. There's something so grotesque about it, like a glass menagerie or an animal farm, except they're humans and no human deserves this.

The only thing Brits can do is laugh and this is the only thing I still turn to them for. Laughter comes in print and television and discs of various sorts. They still live in a sea of words with Eddie Izzard putting them together better than most. Izzard's black-rimmed eyeballs swing while his lipsticked mouth widens into an impossibly huge grin and he says the word *"Az-er-bai-jan"* and I could eat the syllables. He says his standup is just him standing up talking nonsense. People pay for British nonsense. They envy it and yearn for it.

Yet it's a sad thing to roll about as I watch a once-great nation's biggest export—its humour. Besides guns, tanks and fighter jets, I mean.

What a loathsome country. What an awful place it is. I shan't see it again in my lifetime.

Falling in Love with France

Or why France gets me hot

 Trust me to enshallow my love. But I fell in love with France because of the sunlight hitting the Seine in a certain way as I sat at a café drinking table wine. As usual, I qualified my love and this is why I am not what they call a "fun" person. Perhaps the sun is glinting off the corpses of the two hundred Algerians tied up and dumped in the Seine to drown in the riots of 1961, I thought. But I still fell in love.

I had a very good therapist, who is still sort of on-call for me, and she believed in God. I can't be doing with

God, so she asked me to name what I would look to for guidance. And I said the feeling I have when I sit in a café in Paris. I am not myself, I say. I am seated. I do not stir. I ponder. My heart beats slowly. I don't leap to my feet for some suddenly necessary task. I am simply there.

We couldn't ask "How Heather feels in a Paris café" for guidance, so she translated this feeling as "the goodness of life," and that's what we looked to for wisdom. It's a good thing to pray to pleasure, correct?

You shouldn't have to fly across an ocean to have a moment of being. Ideally you'd have it in the bath, and it would also be cheaper and kinder to the earth's atmosphere. Nevertheless in Paris I am the person I wish to be and the hell with faking it the other fifty weeks of the year.

Adam Gopnik says that France does the great and the small, the grandiose and the minuscule. Think of the boulevards and the ancient buildings. Then think of the care with which the lady behind the counter in a shop wraps your inexpensive purchase. Small things matter too. No other country seems to manage this combination well.

The Americans can embark on nothing huge without a consequent disaster that spells death for many. They can't even build a levee properly any more, yet they once built the Hoover Dam. As for small things, all encounters with officialdom are tiny stupidity fests and their low culture is just a big load of ham, a salted crusty pink eraser from which you get scrapings.

Big and small. It works. French history has its moments of great shame, although they seem to have fewer moments of great glory, or *"gloire,"* as the French say with great seriousness. There aren't as many "fuck you" moments in French history as there should be. They were desperately awful colonists, although not as cruel as the Belgians, and they blew up the *Rainbow Warrior,* plus there's a dreadful history of nuclear testing. They always call it "testing." Nuclear power failed the test. No one mentions that, particularly the French.

And their novels are laughable. But so are everyone's. Where's Zola when you need him?

But when it comes to beauty, to food and sex and the pleasures of being alive, the French have written the history. Furthermore, when the history became shabby at the edges, brave people in the *terroir* movement declared they would maintain their farmland, their countryside, their food and their genius for blending rural life with wild life. I don't know if they will win, but what a people.

And when the government tells French workers to kiss ass, they learn to regret that decision they made to finally return cobblestones to the roads that had been paved since 1968. The French will lob their stones, the poor will torch cars; they will all make their feelings known with great certainty.

The citizens of Canada and the United States, not so much.

I understand that France is a strictly ordered and closed society. I understand that difficulty. But I could read any book there in public without being mocked for intellectual pretensions. I tell you, read your Walter Benjamin behind closed doors if you are in North

America. As a matter of fact, the U.S. government will track your purchases on Amazon. Book purchasing would be dubious in the first place, and then I made the gaffe of sending books to Canadian Muslims jailed without trial or even charge after they may have done something or not. Amazon sent the books to the jail. Now our spy agency has banned all gifts of books. These jailed men may not read.

Imagine being on a hunger strike without a book.

That is why France is so intense for me. Good food, good bookstores, wonderful fashion with a strictness about it that means that expenditure doesn't count for everything, wonderful smells and a precision about everything from the materials of storefronts to the colour of the cobblestones. You are surrounded by aesthetic statements. Yes, you leave central Paris and you see dubious aesthetic statements as well as poverty.

But there is a central theme to which the French try to hew. *Liberté, égalité, fraternité,* even if they fail at it. In Canada, it is peace, order and good government, and we try although we fail.

"Est-ce que je suis plus agée pour cette . . . ?" I asked a salesgirl in Galeries Lafayette about a Versace knockoff with a corset tied with eight metres of flesh-pink ribbon. *"Non, pas du tout,"* she said, looking bewildered at the question. It's not age, it's the look.

France is a personal country, an insertion, a core. I understand their language, and find little humour in their daily lives, certainly not the kind that enlivens Britain. But there's something deep and powerful in the French that

I admire. I wish I could live there. But then the illusion of glamour would be gone. There is no such thing as glamour. Let me repeat that. There is no such thing as glamour. Up close, it vanishes.

I would not want my love of France to vanish. It's an evanescent thing, even now. So two weeks a year will do me. Calvinism suits for the rest of the time, a contrast to that fullness and beauty, to that goodness of life.

Fear Festival

If you weren't worried enough, wallow in this

There are so many things we either fear or are expected to fear now. And this is such a commonplace, a staple for stand-up acts, that I would even hesitate to write about it were it not that no one has yet published the full list.

Be vigilant, be very very vigilant. Watch out for grape-fruit juice, which is exquisite on its own but boosts the intensity of some medications so much that it is like a lit match tossed in the gas tank of your stomach. Same for Tylenol No. 3. Same for SUVs, if you are a pedestrian, since you will be crushed under the wheels rather than thrown onto the windshield of a sedan and into the sky, dead either way, but still. Phthalates (the *p* is silent as in *pthysis* and *ptarmigan,* but you knew that) in plastic and nail polish are dangerous, as are pesticides and fertilizers (the latter causing cancer in small children). Microparticles in skin cream that in the course of smoothing and beautifying invade the skin's natural defences and do untold damage inside the body. Flu vaccines in a tiny percentage of cases can leave you paralyzed for months. Flu vaccines that are still made with thimerosal, a mercury preservative included to make more money for the vaccine-maker—think big-box bulk vaccine injected into little Jimmy—may change your child's brain, planting autism. Every bit of the perfect purple flower monkshood is poisonous as hell, but you may not be able to identify it in your garden. Don't inhale carcinogenic fumes from your new flooring. *E. coli* is a danger, as are viruses like avian flu, West Nile, and human papilloma.

There are illnesses that have no symptoms. Take chlamydia.

JFK had chlamydia, which causes premature birth, stillbirth or fatal chlamydial pneumonia in infants. I doubt that Jackie would have had him tested before every sexual encounter, even if he had agreed to stop fucking "strange ass," as he called it, every second day. Thus, we must wonder whether the stillbirth of Arabella and the premature birth and subsequent death of Patrick were caused by JFK. Good thing I warned you. Also, don't injure your back in a sexual encounter and wear a neck brace if there is a chance that you will be assassinated. Make sure you can slide down with ease in your open-top limo.

Watch that mole. Also watch for moles of the rodent kind for they will destroy your lawn and may carry diseases such as hantavirus. Wild mice do this too. Don't let small children eat while travelling in the car, as each crumby, jam-laden, french-fry-baited seat will be a comfortable mouse bedroom.

Imagine being well into your meal when you see one of humanity's Most Hated enter the restaurant and be seated, thus presenting the huge moral dilemma of whether to throw a hot beverage into Henry Kissinger's toad face and be ejected screaming insults, or worse, not to. Worse that that, you are dining alone and no one will ever know of your cowardice.

You go into a washroom, which unknown to you is a hangout for anonymous gay trysts. You have difficulty urinating and your penile machinations are misunderstood by the undercover police officer coming out of a stall. Herbicides are bad.

For reasons you can no longer quite remember, you vilify and slander a wealthy European banker, who fights back valiantly and clears his name, causing you to lose your job running a huge credit card corporation. But the experience wounds the banker so badly that when his bodyguard sets his boss's apartment on fire to impress people with his talent for rescue, the banker is too paranoid about kidnappers to flee and thus burns to death. You knew you were an evil bastard but now you're a murderer too. You become a recluse in your home. One night fire breaks out. Ha ha.

You have your breasts reduced (or perhaps just the one; see below) but your removed and re-attached nipples don't take. They rot and fall off. An air conditioner might fall out of a six-storey window onto your head. You get talked into a colonic irrigation, but you choose a new spa (if the spa realm can be said to get that internal) where they use too great a volume of water and something hidden but crucial ruptures. You die, in great pain, yes, but the embarrassment is worse. Other people just go to the toilet. What, that wasn't an option? Because it's an option for seven billion other people. Think of that as the bright light approaches you. Or is it you heading toward the bright light? Either way, you're dead.

You attend the Sweetwater, Texas Jaycees rattlesnake roundup where six thousand pounds of rattlesnakes are caught, killed and eaten. You are crowned queen. Festival queen Miss Snakecharmer Scarlett Steakley skins a rattlesnake as part of her regal duties and gets covered in snake blood. (How often is one honoured and asked to peel a serpent? I mean, you already got the prize.) You scream, quiver with fear, vomit, can't eat for a week and are never quite the same again. You are worse, I mean.

Falling asleep in front of the television: It could mean you have sleep apnea, which means you experience lengthening periods in the middle of the night where you stop breathing, which deprives your brain of oxygen and slowly makes you stupid while killing you, and you're the last to know because by then you're already hopelessly stupid.

Avoid the Seventies Revival: If you are wearing poly-ester clothing when your plane explodes, your clothes will melt onto you, making it impossible for you to sur-vive your burns. In a repellent episode of grotesque intrusion into the life story of a celebrity who has given me nothing but pleasure, I tracked down the FAA report of the 1974 Eastern Airlines air crash that killed the father and two older brothers of the great satirist Stephen Colbert. The idle chatter of the experienced, alert flight crew caused them to ignore repeated signals that they were flying far too low as they approached the airport. Many passengers burned to death because their trendy clothes melted. I feel ashamed that I sought out this information on the accident that ruined the life of ten-year-old Stephen and I do not like myself at all. So watch out for the Internet turning you into a nasty piece of work. It happened to me. See? It just happened to you too 'cause you read this.

Don't smoke. There are cancers and there are can-cers. Throat cancer is one. You can end up having your tongue removed and being fed through a tube, and you'll allow this knowing that you will still die. This happened to John Diamond who loved his wife Nigella Lawson and their two children so much that he didn't care about being a humble, pretty corpse. It's a death I wouldn't have wished on Slobodan Milošević. So don't smoke. Even dying of drink won't be as bad.

Unplug your office paper shredder before you clean the blades. I didn't once, and I already had a husband who cut off his finger with his own self-wielded secateurs because he was simultaneously pruning and thinking about his impossible teenager, and yet I still didn't unplug the shredder first. I've seen the end of a finger slowly rot, for God's sake. I know whereof I speak.

The following things have been suggested, perhaps by charlatans, to be associated with breast cancer: asymmetrical breasts, the compression of breast tissue by bras, hormone therapy or the lack of hormone therapy, relatives with the disease. So either expand or shrink a breast, go braless, and drop your cancerated mother. She's dead tuh me, as Tony Soprano would say.

The presence of even the slightest glimmer of light or electrical devices in our bedrooms as we sleep is said to shorten our lives. For it is not natural for man to have light during his sleeping hours. I do wonder about cavemen and their fires. Perhaps they were already on the long light slide to an early death. Who needs to know when it's three in the morning? Stomp that glowing clock.

We will not even discuss the damage cell-phone use may inflict on the brain, but the concomitant traffic dangers are likely just as significant. Don't drive while talking to a disembodied voice. As well, don't wear an iPod while jogging on the street, although heaven knows why you are not using the sidewalk. You are running disabled by music. An ironic way to die.

Don't sit under your chimney. It may collapse, wiping out your family. This happened in London, Ontario. Let elevators have their way. Fighting them may lead to decapitation. It does so relatively infrequently considering the time we spend half-on, half-off the elevator, but stay alert. Up or down, it doesn't matter, as long as all of you goes up or down.

Wear heavy gloves when gardening. An errant thorn could cause, and has caused, the loss of many a hand.

Photograph your handymen. Forty years later, your children may discover the Boston Strangler standing behind you in the kitchen with his workmate. If you are the writer Sebastian Junger, you will get a very unusual book out of this brush with death. But that is by the by. My advice is take a snapshot. Once you have photographed him, you have evidence that makes him unlikely to kill you, unless he is driven into a sudden uncontrollable rage. Be polite. Offer herbal tea, not coffee, to your workmen. Or lemonade.

Beware stalkers, especially if you are British politician Mo Mowlam who helped bring peace to Northern Ireland. As a beautiful young student at the University of Tallahassee, she was stalked by Ted Bundy, who went on to strangle, bite, sodomize and smash in the heads of several students there. You have a duty not just to yourself but to your fellow man. And even if your future contains only a disastrous marriage, hateful children, a job at a call centre and a sad hobby like scrapbooking your series of failures, lock your door anyway.

Never volunteer for a drug trial unless the drug has been tested rigorously on animals, and in similar quantities, and all procedures have been followed. Make those procedures your bible. Or else your immune system will explode as did those of several young volunteers in a British hospital and your head will literally expand while you scream for help. At the very least, you will lose your fingers and toes. Furthermore, use your wiles to get into the control group that is given placebos, there's a clever boy.

Eat ginger to prevent ovarian cancer. Or don't. Scientists disagree over whether it provides the faintest help. Same with ginseng, echinacea, green and other special teas. If you have a vasectomy, have a follow-up test to see if it worked. They often do not, Daddy. Then check for prostate cancer, to which vasectomies may be linked. Or not.

If you have a heart transplant, keep your old heart in there, just in case. You've got room. It can work out real well. And you can get the old heart restarted. This is true.

Don't sit on a toilet in the washroom of a dodgy-looking building without checking for rats. Dan Aykroyd didn't check. It was a *huuuuge* rat, he said. Also, if you are kidnapped, beware of Stockholm Syndrome. Think about it. Does this man who has you in manacles truly have your best interests at heart? I would just stay away from Sicily altogether, or Brazil. If you are in Brazil, do not be a destitute street child. Your fate is written in tears already cried. I am crying now. Marry the offspring of Melinda and Bill Gates. Life will be spectacular in a good-quality-sneakers kind of way.

Don't be bitten by sandflies. There's one kind of *visceral leishmaniasis* which is always fatal unless you get to a hospital fast for a month of injections. It eats your spleen and liver. The second kind destroys the mucous membranes in your nose, mouth and throat; the third just gives you big obvious sores. Sandflies hardly sound dangerous. They are. Get a mosquito net with a really fine mesh.

Be very upset during your pregnancy. Add stress to your life by watching speeches by George W. Bush. Argue with your husband or leave him—poverty is the greatest stressor of all. Stress during pregnancy is said to result in children developing at a faster rate, perhaps the result of all that fight-or-flight cortisol leaking from mother to fetus. Although I'm trying to imagine the kind of woman who would be utterly calm through a pregnancy.

Have many boy-children, thus making it more likely that younger sons will be gay. Scientists say that the "maternal memory" means the womb becomes increasingly hostile to those things with a Y chromosome. As it delivers male after male, it attempts to become immune to boys. Proof can be found in stuff found in the folds of the placenta. Gays in the family means that at least some of your children will behave in a civilized fashion and will assure you of companionship in your older years. Alter that will now.

Here's the latest on prostates: The BBC advises men to drink an eight-ounce glass of pomegranate juice each day. (But only if they have prostate cancer, I hasten to add.) "Pomegranates: the fruity panacea," read the site's dreadful headline. And even then, men won't be terribly motivated after they've hammered their seven-thousandth pip and the kitchen looks like someone's lungs exploded outside their body. To accompany the story, the BBC had a photograph of huge off-white balls. Jesus, that's what a sick prostate looks like? I always thought they were like a little broad-bean. But it turns out the picture was of sickly unripe pomegranates. Good luck with your juicing, men.

I'd continue, but you get the picture.

The People I Detest

*I know what you're thinking, she can't get that in one
essay but see, there's the magic of categories*

SUBSET: THE I-FAIL-TO-SEE PEOPLE

If there's one phrase that sums it up, and there is, it is "I
fail to see . . ." Since I live in Canada, this is usually followed by "the humour of . . ." and if it's a newspaper I've
written something for, "Heather Mallick's recent remarks
regarding. . . ."

My recent remarks embrace a multiplicity of things
but what they all have in common is that a certain type of
reader took them deadly seriously and wrote to complain

that I apparently did not.

Now it is a law that only mad people write to newspapers or TV stations to complain. I'm not quite comfortable with this law given that over the past few months I have occasionally felt a passion about something and considered writing a heated letter to a newspaper about it, something beyond "We moved the mailbox to the side of the house last week. Can your delivery people grasp that now?"

Having once edited the Letters page of that under-cooked tabloid *The Toronto Sun,* I know about mad people, and I don't wish to be one. But the fact that I occasionally think of joining their ranks means a) they're not all *that* mad and b) I am quicker to anger now. Furthermore, I am getting older like a pet, i.e., seven years have passed for every birthday cake I've had presented to me (here's a housekeeping tip: icing sugar's fine, but mousse cakes sieved with cocoa should never get a hearty blow, just a little something my carpeting and I have learned over the years) and I'm a coffin-dodger whose clothes are getting baggier and beiger by the minute. I both irritate the world and am irritated by it. I irritate the hell out of myself. (Here's another housekeeping tip: there's a place and an outfit suitable for spraying black Suede Renew on Christian Louboutin pumps, and indoors while wearing the pumps isn't it, when will I learn that?)

Look how hard I try to make myself useful to you. I'm old in mind but I'm sweet and handy as a chunk of apple in a bricklike bag of brown sugar. (That tip actually works; don't say I never taught you anything.) There, I've softened you up.

In truth, aside from politics and the coming destruction of the planet, I have no problem with the way the world is headed. It's better and offers infinitely more opportunities for pleasure and adventure than when I was a child twitching the rabbit ears on the TV.

But I still want to write these letters. Then I read the letters that are written to me and the humourless editors of whatever I'm writing for, and I realize that there's a phalanx of crazed, spittle-spraying, damaged and dangerously un-straitjacketed people out there with nothing better to do than complain about their own wildly incorrect interpretations of what I wrote, having convinced themselves that I will be deeply moved by their complaints.

And sometimes I *am* deeply moved. To write back. And there the trouble begins.

I once wrote a brief shopping column. One week I did four hundred words on children's toys. They should be wood, I said, and not just because wood is chic in toyland. I could give a toss about fashion, allegedly. (I am under the impression that I am not shallow. I could be wrong about this.) Wood is not intrinsically more educational than any other material unless you're teaching your toddler about different kinds of wood, i.e., This is oak, my child, good English oak bought in Hamleys. It was Dutch elm disease that destroyed the superficial good looks of the American small town, well, that and big-box stores and the curse of the automobile but that is by the by. What matters is that when you throw that wooden toy at Auntie

Heather's head, it dents (her head *and* the toy) but you can't say that of plastic.

No, cheap plastic toys made by desperate underage factory slaves (very much like you, my little Alexandra) in China will not dent. But these toys will dry out and split. Worse, they will stain with the plethora of substances you insist on introducing into the living room. A living room is not a place for paint or jam, my child; it is a place for reading and contemplating, or perhaps watching an improving David Attenborough documentary on bird life.

Then the child hits me, hard this time.

I bought a toy kitchen for my niece. It was like a little phone box, but with counters, ovens, microwaves, pots and cutlery, all made of plastic. She loved it and I was, by design and by far, the most popular relative that Christmas. But when I visited next Christmas, I wrote, the play kitchen was broken in six places and irretrievably stained. It looked, I wrote, like the kitchen of an alcoholic.

I then received a letter from an aggrieved man who told me that he was an alcoholic and that his Jenn-Air kitchen was immaculate, positively gleaming. I owed alcoholics, who have struggled to overcome their disability, an apology for impugning their household maintenance.

I wrote back instantly, of course, saying, Dear Sir, Are you certain you weren't drunk when you wrote this?

The guy then sent his letter and my reply to the editor, who insisted that I apologize. I think I did too, for the sheer fun of repeating the line about him being drunk, and said alcoholics are the cleanest, tidiest people I know. It's so funny watching them at Christmas as their faces go numb and they pour an entire drink on their shoes under the impression it is flowing down their little red lane. These people are nature's hygienists. Okay, I didn't put that last bit in the letter.

I am invariably harangued by readers when I write about mental illness, pets and "supporting our troops" in WhereverTheFuck. What I resent and can't say is that I have seen more mental illness than they've had hot dinners, and that is because I venture out of my home where the madmen roam and they clearly do not. It is my job to get outside. It isn't pleasant, but it is always sick-making in an interesting way, especially if you can get a halfway entertaining/useful column out of it.

I remember spending a week trying to track down a cell-phone company that was selling ring tones that were the sound of a woman crying out as she was kicked in the face with a leather boot. After a week of being avoided by a huge company that operated by phone (its public relations people invariably answered the phone with a nervous "How did you get this number?"), I finally screamed at a voice-mail that they'd be sorry, dickless wonders.

Then, and this was both funny and horribly mortifying, I had to write to two men at this awful company and assure them that they had generative organs. Big ones. The editor took that bit out. Which is good, because everyone at this cell-phone company was a misogynist and utterly devoid of dick, so why pretend?

At the time, I did feel guilty because I think it's wrong to disparage men by referring to their genitals.

But this was my problem. Nothing was ever funny to a Canadian, ever. I started to think that Canadians had no sense of humour, and then I realized that it was only Canadian letter-writers who had no sense of humour. Everyone else in Canada was fine, which is why they hadn't written to me. They either saw the humour or hadn't read the column or they were busy with their lives and didn't have the time to witter away to a complete stranger about personal assemblages of resentments built up over the decades.

The thing they didn't know was that I was by nature a polite person. I always apologized after losing my temper. Losing your temper is a failure by definition, I think. It's my dream to be a calm person. I have long known I will never achieve this dream, but now I can see that I won't even be able to build a facade.

Even humourless Canadians started to look good to me after I appeared on *The O'Reilly Factor,* that spewing-on Murdoch-owned Fox News, by that awful loofah-penis yelly-man Bill O'Reilly. He's such a disgrace that Stephen Colbert based an entire show, *The Colbert Report,* on Comedy Central parodying the idiocy, arrogance and dopey cruelty of O'Reilly.

But I was being interviewed by O'Reilly on my welcoming American draft dodgers to Canada. Non-violent, thoughtful young people come here in great numbers, I said. O'Reilly hated this, wanting them all in prison being sodomized by white supremacists, but what he hated more was that I had clean hair, pearl earrings and perfect teeth and I was calling myself a socialist.

I was aiming to show O'Reilly viewers that a socialist could be civilized and reasonable. I imagined his
audience as cave-dwellers who dealt with excretion
by getting down on all fours and letting loose like an
animal. I was right about that last bit, of course. You
would not believe the e-mail I got. These men mentioned their yearning to bend women over logs and
make them squeal like pigs. Worse, they wanted to do
this to these draft dodgers and their wives, some of
whom were *not white,* which was beyond the pale in their
eyes, one might say.

E-mail itself is odd by its very nature. What happens
when your job consists of sitting at home writing is that at
some point you become pathetic enough to make e-mail
friends. I have met almost none of these people, although
they'll show up on book tours and after a speech and they
seem normal and nice. But the problem is that they have
become my social circle. It is not normal to have a social
circle you haven't met.

Inevitably some of them are pedophiles, disappointed to discover that you are a crone of forty and have
no intention of bringing your stepdaughters to meet them
in a coffee shop at 7 a.m. To them, I'm Lolita's mother.

My, we have drifted far from our original topic.
Because people who write to newspapers to complain
about something pointless and daft (if it has a point and
makes sense, they rarely write, why would they. Their
world is rational and filled with productive activities) are
a tiny subset of our original target: People I Cannot Stand.

SUBSET: PLEASURE VAMPIRES, OR PEOPLE WHO
BLOODSUCK THE JOY OUT OF LIFE

It starts with parents and teachers, of course. The thing about the U.S. TV show *Malcolm in the Middle* is that eleven-year-old Malcolm, who turns to the camera with a horrified, bewildered, appalled expression every time an adult says anything adult, has it right when he says the only good thing about childhood is that it ends.

After I finished childhood, I went through years of eating a joy sandwich, mashing and slurping away, not even wasting time on whoever was staring at the juice running down my chin and the lumps of avocado on my lips. (Avocados are made out of fruit fat. Coconuts are crunchy fruit fat. Macadamia nuts are kernel fat. Eat them and see if I'm right.) What was staring at me was my own face in the mirror, inevitably growing older and disapproving of my own pleasure. Other people's pleasure, fine. But my own? For several years, I became my own mother. Oh, I was hard hard hard on myself.

I still am, but I can brush it off more easily now. That's thanks to my new thing. I now notice other people's tight, pursed little mouths and take enormous joy in that. When you hit forty, you increasingly cease to care what other people think. And when someone tells you about their upcoming colonoscopy and the process one has to go through to make it possible for the clinic staff not to simultaneously vomit and faint, and on which they are now embarking and not sparing you any details, you encourage them.

They're such good copy, see?

Someone will be babbling about internal sluices and dousings, and how the worst thing is seeds because the clinic literature emphasizes that it can ruin, just ruin, expensive snaky machinery, apparently. Instead of saying, "You are sucking all the joy out of my life," you take notes. You can make leading remarks like, "I take it you shouldn't eat corn. Them kernels is big. Would you have to buy them a new $178,000 machine or do they just accidentally perforate you in revenge?"

What I'm saying is, turn the tables. In the course of a day, you will meet one or seventeen or 220 joy vampires. And when you were in your twenties, mashing your face into your joy sandwich (yes, since you ask, in university I once got high, hopped in the bath and ate a huge plate of spaghetti; it was massively enjoyable), you didn't notice them. In your thirties, these people brought you down. Hit forty and you'll be using a mental tape recorder.

Thank God I'm not like them, you'll be saying. (This is intended to comfort younger readers. Hope it helps.)

My mother, who loves me and whom I love, each in our own profound and unsaid way, used to crush me with a remark. She does it to this day, and with great skill, I must salute her for that. It is always intended to be helpful. It always hurts. My husband says this "nurturing" skill is in fact natural and comes strung in the blood with motherhood. I then make taut remarks about a different version of disconnection between fathers and daughters. Fathers don't attend their daughters sufficiently to note exactly which spot between the ribs is best for the slipping of the knife and if you want to take pride in that, go right ahead. This debate continues into the evening.

My husband is a carnivore, as am I, but we both like our meat rare. Sometimes we'll be in the midst of one of these discussions—he had a sunlit childhood; I did not— and I'll look at the platter on which rests the roast and the thing will be leaking blood. I like my meat bleu. It's a bowl of blood. (Often there's a crazy salad too.) And the discussion of daughters and mothers and men and what is done to girls and women goes on, and then my husband cuts me another piece of bleeding protein.

To this day, family dinner and the depiction of family dinners leaves me in a state of delight and horror. When the camera drew back and gave us the still life of the family eating together in the great 2006 comedy *Little Miss Sunshine,* I noticed people in the theatre wincing and moving back in their seats along with the lens. See, there was a time when this would have appalled me. All family dinners are appalling to all who were once children.

But now I suck it up. My dinner mirrors the subject under discussion, as well as my feelings. When I was a child, my father, who loved hunting, would come home with a chopped-up moose or deer which he would then cut into smaller pieces which my mother would bag and label for the freezer. I saw none of this. But I remember the house reeking of blood for a week. I imagine the Dick Cheney household being very much like this.

Blood memories. A glass of Jackson-Triggs Merlot— am I the only one who thinks red wine is blood by the glass?—and we have a merry time of it. I knew from a young age, or whatever age it is when you figure out that women have children, that I was not going to do the womanly thing. Other women complain that there is intense social pressure on them to have children, and since I have never felt this pressure, I wonder—is it me? Perhaps people have been pressuring me for years by asking me if I have children and if not yet, then when, and I am so nest-rested in my childhood decision that it has all sailed right past me. When people ask me a personal question, I just assume it's related to some neurosis of their own.

The first reason I never had children is that they hurt coming out. I remember my father, an obstetrician/gynecologist, having been out delivering a baby all night and complaining the next day that he had injured his hand pulling the baby out. *He* complained. Imagine what the mother felt. And no, I don't expect it helps one bit to have your vagina switch identities and suddenly become a "birth canal."

My father's complaint made me think of that British TV show about a vet in Yorkshire, Trooble at 'Cow it was called—no, *All Creatures Great and Small,* and Robert Hardy always had his hand up to the elbow in a cow's back passage. I remember being puzzled when I heard for the first time about gay men fisting in New York and then remembering when the calving went wrong.

Second, I'd be a dreadful mother. Overprotective, yet not admiring myself enough to allow the child to resemble me, I can imagine my poor kid crawling away from me, refusing to wear the clothes I selected, learning to conceal her feelings, growing up to be, like me, an appalling combination of socialist and snob and in other words, never winning. I would love to be that relaxed, casual, oblivious type of mother but think of what you've read of me so far. I can't be that.

Third, I had a miserable childhood. I never remember being hugged by my mother. Being a weirdly self-confident young person, I neither noticed nor cared. But after forty, it struck me as truly odd that I am so physically affectionate with other humans without having had any training as a child. Perhaps I had seen people embracing on TV. Ah, so that's a bear hug.

So what does my mother do? In a casual phone conversation this year, she said, "You know I've been thinking and I can't remember ever hugging you when you were little. I must have been a bad mother." You can see why I love her. She said this unprompted. She's nice.

I was completely sucker-punched, left holding a non-anecdote. "You're right," I said. "You never hugged or kissed me," and then I fell over myself saying that she'd had a tough time as a mother. She was stressed beyond belief and was very ill most of the time, often hospitalized and in great pain. "You did the best you could," I said. "God, you were so sick. It terrified me. Don't worry about it. You were fine."

So the grievance of decades was settled. Done. She did her best. What more can you ask? I was entirely sympathetic, especially since my mother did have a hard time in the early part of her marriage, always stuck in some godforsaken part of the world and I mean places that could only be reached in summer by paddle steamer. She prefers older children and I wouldn't have wanted to be stuck in a house with me as a baby either. I bet I was a high-maintenance infant, and since I know I was a nightmare teenager, the in-between years can't have been grins and giggles. Americans spend billions in therapy over the question of a legacy of being loved or unloved. My mother, who has never sought therapy—she does not know what it is—figured out that she had never led me to believe I was loved. So she apologized, I was charmed silly, and that was it: one grievance down and maybe one more to go.

She then mailed me a large cheque.

I'm an acceptable stepmother. I threw myself into it from the first time I saw those two girls, and when they come over for dinner now, I get maudlin over the elaborate dinners their father cooks them and remember what chubby little cuties they were in Grade One. Not surprisingly, they don't come over much. Imagine how much worse it would be if they'd come out through my "birth canal." Man, they'd owe me. As it is, they owe me nothing and yet I cling to an invisible debt.

Their side of the family is yelly. Mine is not. I prefer yellers. It seems more honest. Isn't it better to be sixteen and scream at your mother that she never hugged you as a toddler than to wait for forty resentful years for her to mention it over the phone, casually collapsing your house of resentment cards?

Now, rather than seeing an argument as a bloodletting, I see it as artwork and therein lies pleasure. I love still lifes. That's some nice crockery, I'll say admiringly of

Giorgio Morandi who basically paints white jugs. But the still lifes I really love are the Northern Flemish painters of the sixteenth century, who really go at it. They painted slaughtered birds and serpents—Metsys was the best—and these things were splattered all over the table. Still life is not an adequate phrase; still bleeding would be more like it.

I'm all for vegetarianism. It sounds terribly fine. But not being a cook, and since left to my own devices I will eat cheese for breakfast, lunch and dinner, I'm a vegetarian by default. Someone in my house keeps roasting bleeding haunches for me—I mean, roast oxtail—for dinner. Seriously. You don't know where it's been. But you can imagine. It was the tail of an ox. Or is this a euphemism? I can just see the fly-ridden thing flapping in the pasture. But now it's skinned and doubtless marinated and I am sitting with my husband, eating the swatter from a cow's ass and talking about people who suck the joy out of life.

I bet you thought I couldn't find my way home.

When I was a young girl, I developed starter breasts. I remember a girlfriend at school suggesting I should be wearing a bra and then literally biting her tongue, as someone as hopelessly uncool as me could not manage such a thing. So I summoned up the blood and asked my mother for a bra.

She looked at me and said in her coldwater Glaswegian accent and a note of what I accept thirty years later was indeed genuine, not faked, puzzlement, "What good would that do?"

How do you answer that? *I'll get practice? All the other girls wear one and I'll fit in? Oh, go on, be a sport?*

Instead, I melted into a small puddle. A year later, I developed breasts out of nowhere—indeed I have them to this day and take them with me everywhere I go—and I dealt with it somehow. Girls need an adviser. The straps on the bra I eventually obtained used to keep falling off my shoulders. It took me years, I swear, to figure out that the little buckle on the strap means it's adjustable . . . oh never mind.

I won't tell you the story of my mother's reaction when I got my first period. I mean, you can guess. But I always envied Carly Simon, the singer who is the love of my life and a big hunk of my personal soundtrack, because when she got her period, her mother took her up to the deck at the top of the house and together they saluted the moon with a glass of wine and a toast to men. (Simon's mother was a real piece of work, by the way, a mother-lode, so to speak.)

Whereas my initiation involved paper grocery bags and bulk purchases of menstrual pads (in the early seventies, they still came with belts you could buy in grocery stores) that my mother collected from a catalogue delivery outlet.

Talk about sucking the joy out of things, I have a Great-Aunt Mavis who is a maestro, a Tenszing, an Olympic champion Mark Spitz (who's a dentist now) at it. She is fantastically unkind to my mother, and that I cannot forgive. She's a Razorblades Heidi, a holder of grudges, a hater of small children, the wettest blanket in my family, which is saying something dire indeed. Her grown-up children are the dullest people I know. Even their toddlers are dull. Is that even possible?

She'll discuss her approaching vacation. Japan? Norway? Dare I suggest India? "Well, if it's as hot as it was in 1952, they can keep it," she'll say, dismissing the entire Indian subcontinent with a wave of her hand. All you can do is gobble silently to yourself—*I imagine it is. I imagine they have kept it. And will continue to keep it. It's not like they've been waiting agog for forty years for you to come pay another visit.* But I don't say this. I just stare at her like Malcolm in the Middle. She's a big mannish woman with cruel hair and a slice for a tongue and frankly I'm frightened.

She's the kind of person who makes fun of retarded children, borderline tormenting them when their parents are looking. She won't let you read the newspaper in her living room because you might get ink on the chesterfield. I would normally sympathize with this, having a touch of cleaning disorder, but in her case, it just means she's too cheap to get her upholstery cleaned. She has one of those houses that are furnished, beyond question they are furnished, but you sit down and think, What now?

There are no bookcases, no snacks or televisual devices or even a magazine or a pet. She's the most *discomfort*-making woman.

SUBSET: NUTTERS

I have a stalker. She used to be my best friend, a loyal, gentle person then, if prone to inexplicable rages that we used to puzzle over. Later, she grew more like a sharpened knife twanging unnervingly, and some years later I dropped her. It gives you no grace to drop someone, but she was too cruel by then to have in the room. It made no difference that she was later diagnosed with a particularly harsh mental disorder. I could no longer cope with her.

The weird thing is that despite the things she did to me (and they were things girlfriends don't do; ask a girl-friend and she'll tell you), the greatest grudge I held against her had to do with gabled roofs. Gables are the upside-down V you see on the roofline of a house. They're there because they repel rain and snow, they look good, and they give you an attic if an attic is what you want. The alternative to gables is flat roofs, brought into fashion by a little shit named Le Corbusier. What ensued was a century of leaking roofs.

I and my nutter gal-pal were riding on a train and I noticed a roofline. I then said something about it being odd that they still clung to flat rooflines in Canada, even when gables were so much more attractive and practical in a snowstorm.

My off-centre friend lost it. Why do you even notice things like that? she hissed. And this is what they mean when they say something takes the cake. I was disgusted. I managed to get through high school without anyone noticing I was brainy (I wasn't that smart in university, so no problems there), but she seemed to think I had made what verged on an intellectual remark. Girls aren't supposed to know about the deterioration of architecture between the two world wars.

Okay, I'm saying it. I dumped a friend over a remark about rooflines. You'd think it couldn't be done, but it can. The fact is, I'm irresistible to nutcases, always have been. And generally, they're women. It's not flattering. They're always damaged people, in some way. What is there in me that calls out to them? I'm sending out "Oh bugger off" thought waves but perhaps Peasblossom (Titania and Oberon's most annoying sprite) has mischievously translated them into "Let us be bosom friends. Literally. Here's some serious glue."

SUBSET: BOOK-HATERS

I used to take great joy in watching the Buffalo, New York real estate channel (until they took it off because no one in their right mind was buying a house in Buffalo, New York, where there are no jobs and nothing to do except self-harm on a Sunday afternoon) because I had a running bet with myself that I would never see a house with a bookcase. And I never did.

If the problem were illiteracy, I wouldn't mention it. But it's not, because what are the odds? I grew up in small northern towns all over Canada and every single one of them had an excellent library even if it was housed in an abandoned gas station. No, the problem is a suspicion of books and people who read them.

I used to be book review editor at a tabloid. They were the happiest working days of my life (and my working life has been a tattered flag of misery; I hate newsrooms) because no editor at the paper had ever read a book and they were much too intimidated to approach or, I imagine, ever read anything I wrote about books. This was not surprising. But I used to get calls from readers who'd say, "That sounds like a great book! Where can I buy that?" And I'd say gently and slowly, "At . . . a . . . bookstore." I'm ashamed that I tell this story as if it were funny.

There was something in those years that felt masturbatory in reading books at the rate I read them, and I read even more of them now. I read so much that I get a federal tax break on my reading glasses. I take great joy in my reading, propping books up on a small pillow on my belly as I lie at 120 degrees on the couch, as though I were feeding the words into my body as well as my eyeballs. I feel like Malcolm. I don't want to be in the gifted program, the Krelboynes, as they were called in the show. I'm not gifted. I'm normal. I wanna be with the other kids. I just have this trick in my brain—I was born smart and I'm ambivalent about it—that only adults are comfortable with. And I secretly think it's worthy, if misery-making.

But the nice thing about adult life is that at some point, it ends.

SUBSET: PEOPLE I CAN'T STAND IN A
GENERAL SCATTERSHOT SENSE

Cheese-paring tippers; people who don't tip chambermaids (vacuuming up your eyelashes is way worse than serving you drinks, buddy); airlines that serve McFood boxes (I don't mind paying, but I'd like something better than a pork-patty melt made with mashed pig vulva); airline passengers who pour Metamucil into their bottled water after dins and shake shake shake; anyone with an SUV; men who drive their Humvees home and let them overhang the lawn; women with handbags Kevlared with chrome holes, buckles, studs and bumpers; women who change their names after marriage (unless original family name horrible, new name is great escape after tunnelling under ze family prison camp walls).

I hate raindrops on roses if they're hybrid roses. I hate brown paper packages tied up with string because modern postal machinery will hook the string and shred your Christmas present. Whiskers on kittens are weird. Are they nerves, and if so, is it an act of torture when the pet groomer trims them? Bright copper kettles are miserable to polish and I know nothing of schnitzel and strudel but it all sounds Teutonic, bloating and not very nice. I have no objection to white dresses with blue satin sashes, but as for snowflakes and silver-white winters that melt into springs, it's the factories of Nazi Germany and its little pal Austria that contributed to the black ball that choked our planet when the Nazis took over, so farewell, Austrian skiing industry.

I don't like George W. Bush's "heh heh heh" and I despise him for resenting Yale for taking him in just because his daddy went there. Take the freebie, George, you took all the other ones. George could have gone to technical college and made a nice living as a panel-beater in a garage, from which people with dented cars emerge with smooth, slick machines that give them a slidy, shiny satisfaction. But no, you had to get back at your dad. What did Iraqis and Iranians ever do to you, George?

I don't like plastic. I like plastic buckets that ease the burden of African women carrying water for miles to their families, but that's only because the men don't bother. Plastic littered the planet with ugliness. I return to my original point: wooden computers, that's the ticket! How about a nice wooden telephone and a wooden bed instead of the iron bedstead thing with perpendicular rails that always traps my head late at night. It's stylish but it could stand some plywood, frankly, Mr. Art Shoppe who sold it to me.

I used to like drugs until they became necessary. I don't mean for actual illnesses, but for coping with life. Is Peter D. Kramer at all embarrassed about *Listening to Prozac?* It never worked out, did it, Peter? We're as miserable as ever. This means that there was something implicitly wrong with your theory.

I had this awful salesman come and sell me new windows for a ridiculous price. In the end he just screwed me. The contract meant nothing to him; the project was a disaster. Such a stickler am I for avoidance that I started using the side door rather than the front door in the porch I had replaced at such expense. Yes, that's a big barrel of nuts, I agree.

But I signed and paid in advance. Do you know why? Because he acted like a person on Prozac who wasn't on Prozac. Or else he was imitating the mannerisms he recalled from the days when Prozac worked. He was chirpy and perky. His voice was artificially high. He said "Gosh" and "Dandy" a lot. All his mannerisms were "up." If I can extend the analogy perhaps a little too far, he was up in the same way that Italian, especially Venetian churches, are always up. The paintings are on the ceilings. Jesus is hovering over the altar right at the very top. As the oboe and the flute rise, your head lifts to see his halo painted gold on the fresco. You come out of Venice with a neck that aches. The doges intended this. People always forced to look up don't look down and see filthy cobblestones and churchmen accepting bribes for a passage to heaven.

In the same way, raising one's voice up and talking optimistically about a new beautifully windowed future distracts you from the contract and the cheque which you sign, not thinking that these lower things mean nothing to the Up Man.

But what do you expect from a guy named T. Randall anyway? I bet he's from Kentucky. Same with those millions of American men with a first name that sounds like a last name. Spencer, Cable, Kendrick, Hayward, Sumner, Fleenor. They're just distracting you horizontally. Look up. Look over there. Look anywhere but where you should be looking.

SUBSET: PEOPLE WITH FURKIDS

The phenomenon of Furkids has probably been around for decades but it hadn't come out of hiding until recently. Old ladies and their hundred or so cats, fur-coated society ladies and their tiny bald doglets, that we knew.

But now that people can choose when to have children and now that old people have been fatally (in the taste sense) encouraged to dress and behave like children (pastel tracksuits and fanny packs, my dear lord) while spending their children's inheritances on cruises and gatherings where they can bore each other like a trepanning instrument, it's time for Furkids. I lay bare our latest societal shame.

Furkids are children. Except they are not human children. They are standard household pets, i.e., cats and dogs, that are dressed, groomed, fed, spoken to and treated like beloved children. They are kids but they have fur and they lick themselves. You'd think the latter would disqualify them, but I asked around and there's your answer as to how people can stand to have dogs in bed with them. Licking is a good thing in this case. Your other question—what about the hair?—shrivels by comparison.

There's nothing wrong with having Furkids while you're waiting to have human children. In fact there's nothing wrong with having them along with your human children or as company when your children have left home. Sorry, I meant there's nothing wrong with having pets. Furkids are not pets. They are hairy children and are treated by their mummy and daddy (never referred to as owners) as such.

This is sick.

Here's how to spot a Furkid. It has its own website. I don't have a website, mainly because the kind of people who tell me I should have one invariably refer to it as a "marketing tool." I'd call it "boasting." So no website for me.

Furkids don't eat pet food. They eat special treats bought at great expense from the local dog bakery. In a world where four billion of our total six are ill-fed to the point of affecting life expectancy, the entire concept of a dog bakery makes me swill with rage liquids. I walk past a canine bakery preferring to think of it as a place where Furkids themselves are baked. This comforts me.

Furkids have cute names. They are never called Spot or Rover. It's always Mrs. Muggles or Clooney or Chewbacca III.

Furkids have wardrobes. By this, I mean matching hat-and-coat ensembles, often in tartan and often matching their parents' outfits, and I don't mean Chewbacca II, I mean Mr. and Mrs. Finnerty next door whose kids left home and never come back to visit. Doubtless the Finnertys have some version of the deep dark family secret that torments everyone else on my street, but I notice that most people's kids still visit, bearing grandkids or grimaces or something, but they're there.

Does it ever occur to the Finnertys that the kids don't visit because they come second to Thatcher Baxter, a small yappy-type dog with a urinary problem that has his parents wringing their hands in a way they never did for young Spencer Finnerty? He has a wife, two children and a secret fear that training for and starting a career in outplacement consulting (he fires people on a contract basis) was the biggest mistake of his life. He cannot talk to his parents about his growing panic, indeed despair. For his parents have transferred their affections to Thatcher Baxter.

I actually know a woman who invited her daughter on a trip to the Bodrum resort in Turkey, tickets bought, itinerary planned. Daughter puzzled, thrilled, possible new relationship with maddening mother, zippety-doo-dah. Then Ma billed her for it. Daughter, who could not afford the trip, paid with postdated cheques and the equivalent of rolls of pennies. Ma then spent precisely twice that much having her Furkid's teeth capped.

Affections? I meant *infections*. Furkids have endless infections. I note this is also true of small children who gobble germs daily. But their illnesses are almost cute. Their button noses run, they cry for mummy, they cling and cuddle.But Furkids get disgusting illnesses, the hall-mark of which is their parents' willingness to treat them at immense cost and talk about them at unspeakable volume. Thatcher Baxter–type Furkids invariably need glands massaged, invariably get damp-ass blockages in the crotch. Whatever goes wrong with them is always foul-smelling and hard to get to. They have elaborate diets and often become obese like their owners.

It's easy to make a dog lose weight. Make him run for his limited Kibbles. But parents of Furkids are as indulgent to their offspring's wants as they are to their needs. Hence, fat cat.

I never notice when animals are morbidly obese as I have no idea what the ideal weight is for seven hundred breeds or mixed breeds of dog or cat. Dalmatians are skinny is about all I know. People with Furkids become medical experts. They're like vets and vets are weird. My girlfriend took her dying dog to the vet (yes, she was terribly sad but she wasn't insane about it) and he actually offered to keep the animal at no cost if he could test a new medical treatment on it. I couldn't tell if it was vile experimentation or an unhealthy attachment to his patients. But I could tell it was somehow inappropriate for little Sparky. So could my girlfriend, and she had the dog put to sleep lest he end up like Terri Schiavo, on life support but looking too good on video to starve to death.

I used to think the worse thing that could happen to a cat was getting run over. That's one reason I don't have a cat. I can't even come to terms with my own certain death, can't seem to plan for it. But way worse things than flattening happen to Furkids.

Furkids get breast cancer, feline leukemia complex, roundworms, hookworms, tapeworms, whipworms, and heartworms. They get fleas and lice, mange and mites, ticks and toxoplasmosis. I don't know what any of this means but it came right off Google. After that came nuttier stuff like websites recommending homeopathic remedies for animals pursued by Big Pharma. I didn't even know animals got vaccinations. But Furkids get them.

Then there's the senior Furkids, whose teeth give out. They take longer naps, their fur turns grey, they get deaf, fat and arthritic and they vote Republican. They pee themselves and you have to get pee samples for the vet by following Thatcher Baxter around with a pie plate. They need special toothpaste, and Furkid parents recommend installing baby-gates so your "senior pet" can't climb the stair, stumble and break a paw. Furkids get better medical care than we do. You know how men won't go to the doctor even when we tell them to, even when the bone is practically piercing the skin? If your husband were a Furkid, not human, that is, he'd go to the doctor every time you recommended it. He'd have no choice. Furkids are permanently in a veterinarian's care. It's not normal. It must be so embarrassing for a male Furkid, because they can't say, Nah, it'll grow back, the way a human husband does.

This is why hairy children are so popular with a certain type of human parent. They do as they're told. They wear what they're given. And they're given Furkid booties, diapers, pyjamas, ponchos, and special outfits in spring and at Christmas.

I give you this from an online pet supply store for the criminally insane: "Tennis anyone? This adorable little tennis dress is the perfect style statement for your pooch. Choose either white & blue or white & pink. Your dog will look like she just came off of the court in this new dog style statement. Tennis ball sold separately."

The site also sells a Happy Trails Plus pet stroller for your obese or non-ambulatory pet (perhaps a new mom!). It looks like a regular human baby stroller but shorter, like a hot-pink ball on wheels.

The site has a section for other types of kids but I don't have the heart. Imagine the kind of clothes they sell for Fishkids.

By the way, Furkids die. If only their Furmoms and Furdads lived in pet years, but no, they live on to buy coffins which look eerily like what you'd purchase for a baby, a human infant, except nicer. Furkids get their own cemeteries. Yes, they take horses. The University of Florida maintains a website offering advice. Parents can call Pet Grief Support Hotlines whose FAQs warn the bereaved not to tell their human kids that the Furkid is only sleeping. Real children often have trouble sleeping after hearing this.

They also answer questions like "When will I feel better?" "How long will I feel this way?" "How will I get over this?"

I hope you never feel better. I hope you suffer forever. I had a part-time dog once. His name was Skipper. We moved away, and I guess he died. He ate dog food. I can still remember how bad he smelled. That was fine with me. He used to hug my leg when I went to school. I guess I'd give my leg to have him back, but that's a stupid idea since he'd be about four hundred years old now, so, unlike you people I'll shut up about him.

He was a great dog, but he was no Furkid. How will I get over this, my ass. Screw you and your dogs with hats. I mean it. Pull yourselves together, for God's sake, and stop making public fools of yourself and embarrassing your pets.

Honestly, Furparents today . . .

Lessing Is More

Why Doris Lessing won't win the
Nobel Prize for Literature

 Each year I stage a
protest at Doris Lessing's failure to win the Nobel Prize for
Literature. It must be said that my protest consists of me
rolling my eyes, perhaps thumping my fist on the table
at dinner during a discourse ignored by all present, and
writing a sarcastic column about the undoubted worthi-
ness of Dario Fo but what were those old Swedes thinking
of that year, et cetera, et cetera. This has little effect.

I am a great worshipper of people whose work I
admire—the living ones include Lessing, musicians Joni

Mitchell, Bruce Springsteen and Kate Bush, the American essayist Anne Lamott, the linguist and political theorist Noam Chomsky, journalists Robert Fisk and Seymour M. Hersh, British novelists Margaret Drabble, Ruth Rendell and Margaret Forster (to name but three of fifty)—but I'm not a fan in the standard sense. Why would I want them to sign my books? They don't know me; I can't pretend I know them.

But it galls me that I had a ticket to a Doris Lessing reading at the Harbourfront Festival in Toronto and on the night I could not bear to go. The thought of all those wealthy intelligent women readers in expensive cloaks of fine Irish wool in the audience was suddenly unbearable. I was too depressed to face Lessing's formidable and indeed admirable fans. Better to stay home in the fetal position with one of her novels and admire her the way a great writer should be admired, with some silent reading. Lessing despises the modern view of "author as personality," and what sane writer doesn't? You may be desperate to get out of the house, but after the first day of the tour, you long for your nest again. You're just a writer after all, a private person. Having done Lessing the favour of not pestering her fifteen years ago, I will not write about the extraordinariness of this woman. Her famous book is *The Golden Notebook* but it was before my time and I cannot warm to it. People shouldn't worry about disliking books widely accepted as great, or avoiding them for decades. They should wait for the stage when they are ready for the book, for it will come. I have read with such excess all my life that I could always use the excuse that I had another book on the go. I didn't know this when I was young, but I would still have plenty of time to encounter the great unread.

My favourite of her novels is *The Summer Before the Dark,* as I find books about chosen solitude very interesting. There is also a passage where the woman protagonist, Kate, stands on a balcony in Spain. Lessing's description of the quality of the darkness makes me shiver. Shakespeare would envy it, and yet Lessing is a writer said not to be a prose stylist, whatever that is.

Then there is the wonderful *The Good Terrorist,* which everyone should read for a level view of oneself when young. I think this last one got her in trouble with the Nobel people. Criticize the young revolutionary at your peril.

But it would never have occurred to Lessing to soften the truth or her own reaction to it.

In Lessing's three-volume autobiography—the third of which was written as a novel in order to spare the feelings of the living, an un-Lessing-like sentiment—she is frequently astonished. And she admits it.

Nothing is more unfashionable than this. I find it astonishing that it is unfashionable to be astonished, but Lessing and I are as one on this, even if we are astonished by different things.

Writing about Lessing offers a wonderful clarity, like a broad sunlit upland where everything is as it seems. She always aims for honesty and very much resembles Woolf, whom she admires, in her effort to pin the feeling or the reason to the page with her pen. Never pretend that something isn't worth having simply because you can't have it, Woolf wrote. That's a Lessing sentiment.

Now eighty-seven, she can shrug a little. But she is still astonished at the cruelty and self-deception of people. And she is still outraged.

Outrage is not allowed.

I am frequently outraged. The outrage is followed by shock when people "tsk tsk" me as though a woman should not be angry about social injustice or some political grotesquerie, some spectacular hypocrisy of the moment. I hate being told to tamp down my voice. This has happened to me a great deal in Canada, where most people are polite and obedient and oblivious and like others to be that way too. So I have often not spoken when I am outraged. This makes me ashamed of whatever editor has shut me up, and it has made me dislike being female.

Lessing wrote a short book in 1987 about the Russian invasion of Afghanistan, the Mujahedin resistance and the resulting flight of four million Afghans to refugee camps on the Pakistani border. The book's title was *The Wind Blows Away Our Words* and every word is written with despair that it will do any good. Lessing begins with a short essay on the lessons of history and how we fail to learn them. And then she tells us about the Afghan people whom she loves and who don't deserve their fate, as if anyone did deserve such horrors.

She writes of her frustration with the ill-informed, shallow, often hopelessly stupid questions of the journalists who interview her. But this has long been a source of complaint for Lessing, that journalists frequently write things that are wildly untrue, not just about her but about everything. Yet they easily could have been fact-checked. Even biographers do this—how could the woman who wrote Lessing's biography without permission have got her daughter's name wrong?—and it is a constant complaint.

That's why Lessing wrote her autobiography, feeling that everyone else could have a go after her death. It is rather exhausting to contemplate Lessing's huge output of novels, short stories, political writing and then expect her to write memoir because someone else would do it so badly, but that is what she did.

In the second volume of her memoirs, which covers her arrival in London from South Africa and the drab fifties, a decade in British life that has been largely ignored, she despairs of reviewers who said she hadn't openly wailed over her decision to leave two children behind with their father and take her son Peter (son of Gottfried Lessing) with her to London. Lessing is astounded. She didn't write about it because to her it is obvious that a woman would suffer over abandoning her children, so much so that she didn't want to waste time on what the reader could take for granted and readily imagine.

This kind of thing doesn't win you points with women-haters, and the press is packed with those. It sometimes does surprise me that Lessing is astonished. I don't subscribe to the notion that children need to be with their mothers. In my experience, they would be better off with other children and supervisory adults; what if the mother does not wish to spend every day and every night with her children? Children and parents can bore each other; what if another adult might do a better job?

But I know this is heresy, and Lessing should know that it is heresy, even if it is true. My mother was temperamentally more suited to older children; we lived in isolated towns. My sister once casually said to me that they should have stopped with her and not continued with me, the youngest. I could only agree. Young mothers are handed impossible burdens. Why romanticize them? But that's another heresy.

Lessing has fought the received wisdom all her life. For instance, she came to be interested in science fiction and eventually wrote a wonderful group of science fiction novels. But to this day, they are largely ignored because the received wisdom is that science fiction is an unworthy genre. But bad writing exists in every genre; why the snobbery this time?

She wrote an extraordinary novel about a fashionable woman taking an old woman under her care. It was *The Diaries of Jane Somers*. I shall not forget the scene where the woman screws up her courage and removes the old woman's weird, multi-layered collection of ancient garments and bathes the accumulated dirt off her body, with warm water and care. It was a heresy itself to write a novel about the old. The received wisdom is that old people are not interesting. But her other heresy was to test the quality of publishing in the early eighties and submit the manuscript to publishers under an assumed name.

She faced rejection after rejection, only a few clever editors noticing that her style had a Doris Lessing air to it. Finally, she declared herself. This heretical test (how dare she play tricks on an industry that has been kind to her?) wasn't aimed at mental laziness or the traditionally sorry state of publishing. Lessing believes what every publisher knows, that there are some books that do not sell many copies, yet their influence is immeasurable. Somehow they set the tone for how people in a country or a culture are thinking about the world. They do this in some magical subterranean way. Yet they matter. Publishers have to fight for such writers and such books.

Someone had to make the point that some books should be published even if they aren't going to make any money. Naturally, only Lessing has the gall.

I suppose here I should provide examples, since Lessing has not. I'm not schooled in this, I think frantically. But I do think that critics rarely refer to the poetry of Margaret Atwood. Yet she is arguably an even greater poet than she is a novelist. Her poems are of a certain style. They resemble those of the great Anne Sexton, for instance. They are very female. They are extremely precise in their language; you could almost call them strict.

But I think they set the definition of what a new kind of poetry by women could be: not obscure, although obscurity is fine; carefully defined, although a wildly flailing poem can be wonderful too; and with an attention to detail that is feminine and often ends in shock.

Lessing is very good about the courage of the young. She began a 1992 short story collection, *The Real Thing,* with the mundanely titled "Debbie and Julie." The runaway Julie gives birth in a dank hut in a back alley in London, following the instructions given to her by a prostitute friend Debbie who took her in. She is kept company in the shed by a tethered starving dog, who scarfs down the afterbirth, Julie's reward to him for his not having bitten her. She then leaves the towelled infant in a phone booth where it is rescued, and returns to her parents' home. Her secret is safe.

Who gives a moment's thought to the Julies of this world? Londoners go about their business, metres away from scenes like this. Urban life has changed little over the centuries.

Lessing can be counted on to be surprising, whatever she reaches for. I have yet to meet a reader who doesn't speak of *The Fifth Child* with awe. A woman and her husband have a perfect family of four. She is pregnant with her fifth. She knows even then that something is very wrong. And she gives birth to Ben, who is strange and unknowable, feral and frightening. Her life is ruined. Her family is fractured. You see this happen in everyday life, but no one writes about that last, single mistake, the child who should not have been, who will not be coped with, who cannot cope with himself.

At the moment, Lessing is unfashionable. She may return to fashion in the way Barbara Pym did in the seventies, named in a list of Britain's most underrated writers. Pym had been brutally discarded in the sixties, but her tragicomic post-war novels of sensible, prudent women have been revived.

I suppose Lessing will become fashionable again when readers realize that *Mara and Dann,* written in 1999, is an accurate prediction of the future as our climate changes according to what poisons we have inflicted on the planet. Atwood's *The Handmaid's Tale* and *Oryx & Crake* predict a political future; Lessing's novel is all about water and heat.

Though I don't know that Lessing wants to be fashionable again. She will be profiled, interviewed, poked and prodded at, and it won't add to the sum of human knowledge. Just read the books. That is all she ever asked, aside from expecting people to be rational, and they won't be, and that's all she wrote.

The Life Wot I Had

Or was that someone else's life altogether?

Someone very clever—
I no longer recall who—has this theory that there is no
such thing as fixed memory. She says that time changes
our memory of events considerably. We must accept this
and agree that our memories are the sum of the actual
event plus the spin we added as the years passed. She says
memory is a collection of versions, and since what we
recall now, in light of our experiences, is arguably as respectable as our interpretation at the time, why not
accept memory as a plastic, not a rigid, thing?

Normally I wouldn't accept this. It happened, it hurt, I built a brick wall around it and I never considered it again. This is the sensible and less painful way to cope with the memory of a bad event.

The problem arises, though, when we study eyewitness testimony in murder trials. As we gain more scientific tools to prove guilt or innocence, eyewitness testimony has become about as respected in a courtroom as phrenology, which was a twentieth-century fad for discovering truths by analyzing the bumps on people's heads.

It turns out that the testimony of even well-meaning white eyewitnesses cannot be relied upon when it comes to identifying an accused person who is black. Whites can't recognize the subtle differences of the black human face. Crudely put, blacks look pretty much alike to them. The same goes for all cross-race identification.

But I'm as convinced as any white granny pointing her shaking finger at the young black man facing her in the courtroom. It was him! Naturally, she is pointing at the Crown attorney.

I can't remember people's names. I can't even remember their faces. Their character and sense of humour are things I recall in a general way. And I can't quote poetry correctly. I could swear that the poet who said we had no time to stand and stare and who was standing on London Bridge saying "Dull would he be of soul" was W.H. Davies. Why would I get that wrong? There's no time crossover between W.H. Davies and Wordsworth.

In a speech I mentioned that the playwright Dennis Potter wrote a play with the wonderful title of *Blue*

Remembered Hills, but an audience member later corrected me. Potter didn't come up with the title. It was Housman. Furthermore, it wasn't about his childhood in the Forest of Arden; it was of course the Forest of Dean, and anyway it was all about an awful childhood sexual memory that doesn't match the beauty of blue remembered hills at all.

Although I remember quoting from *Ulysses* in a column once and I received a letter from a horrible woman accusing me of plagiarizing Tennyson. Imagine the sadness of not knowing that poetry is a common well and Alfred, Lord Tennyson's descendants aren't due royalties and that quoting isn't plagiarizing, I just assumed everyone would recognize some of the most famous lines in the English language not from Shakespeare.

Maybe everything is an immense misunderstanding. Layers of lies upon lies upon mistakes upon misunderstandings form over the years like a coral bed building itself up. This is what makes Google Earth so dangerous. I zoom around the planet revisiting places where I once lived. Places filled with memories perhaps best left alone.

I remember a scene from C.S. Lewis's *The Voyage of the Dawn Treader* where they sailed in the fog past a marooned man. The crew hastened to rescue him, but once on board he warned them to flee. This is the place where dreams come true, he said. Oh goody, they said.

You don't understand, he said. Not daydreams. Dreams.

And everyone gasped and understood, hoisted the mainsail and hustled away.

Google Earth lets you travel with a terrible ease to places you left behind. Normally you would have to gird your loins, make plans, set aside money, make careful maps and then walk down the street past the house where you were abused or the alleyway where you did it standing up with a total stranger or the building where you were stuck in an elevator. That's why you don't go back. It isn't worth the candle.

No rearview mirror, as S. always tells me.

But Google Earth makes it possible. You can do things like revisit everywhere in the world you ever threw up. I suppose that's fun in a peculiar way. You can visit everywhere you ever had sex, if you can remember something resembling an address, or all the places where your girlfriends have been raped. I shudder to think of them ever coming up with this morbid idea, but then they probably feel they can leave it to me. You could visit every one of Barbra Streisand's homes and puzzle as to why one person needs seven places, or in Ted Turner's case, twenty-three and an airplane.

I can track down the Cambodian factory that is notorious for being the worst sweatshop on earth. It produces clothes for the British high street. It has made me very sarcastic about cheap clothes and even less likely to visit Britain, whether this is reasonable or not.

Worse, Google Earth confirmed for me that my childhood memories, unlike the gradually fuzzing memories I accumulate as an adult, are deadly accurate. On Google Earth, I revisited a city where I used to live as a child and tracked each step to school. It was the unhappiest time of my life. I had never thought much of it, and only mentioned it in passing to a therapist once. But I used the cursor to relive that square kilometre of misery, and it was all the same, as if it had been sprayed with a fixative.

It is a wonderful thing to stop painful memories in their tracks. The human mind can accomplish that. What Google Earth is doing is allowing you to return to the dream of childhood, not the lovely bits, but the nightmares. It's like seeing your rapist in court. I have not been raped, but I can imagine that I would never wish to see him again.

Closed-circuit television involves the same traducing of human experience. A British woman was drunk. She was raped on a train platform, her rape filmed by cameras. A man was arrested and convicted even though she fortunately had no memory of the attack. But she was forced to see the video in court and she naturally fell apart. Her life was scarred from that moment on. Before, the alcohol had protected her.

So I don't know about technological tracking devices intruding into my own life. Everyone else is enraged by the government's use of these devices to spy on us. But what horrifies me just as much is that given the chance, such records would allow me to spy on my own past. And we should never be allowed to do that. We should have only our own memories to rely on, dead-on, faulty, whatever. My whole life is online in pictures for the world to see, if the world cared, which it doesn't, and if it knew what it was looking for. Again, it does not.

But I'm naked. I'm stripped and shivering out on the headland.

We move out of small towns to the anonymity of cities to escape this kind of close scrutiny. With all our footsteps on film, we've made the planet not a kindly village but a hideous one.

McLuhan meant us to look at other people, not to neurotically and pointlessly track ourselves.

It is wrong. It is hateful.

How to Ignore Things

It's cheaper than therapy

I'm very good at ignoring unpleasant things. I have to be; there's always something fresh coming up.

But enough about me. Let's talk about the champion of blocking it all out.

If you really analyzed the life of Jacqueline Kennedy Onassis, there's no doubt that she was appalling. Part of it not her fault. It was the era and the social scene into which she was born. You came out of the appropriate vagina, i.e., one linked to a moneyed penis—and if something went wrong, such as your maternal vagina dumping the paternal penis, which is what Jackie's mother did to her alcoholic philandering husband, you spent your youth feeling fragile. You had the name but the mansion only came on sufferance. Janet married an Auchincloss, a good name, but not terribly financially secure.

Basically, Jackie was Lily Bart, the heroine of that Edith Wharton novel that causes any woman without a job to have a mental and emotional collapse, and then go out and get a job.

So Jackie married a philanderer. Her revenge was justified overspending. She spent madly. Then she married Aristotle Onassis, an ugly man with a certain charm that vanished with old age and events such as the death of his son. Jackie spent madly to compensate for the abuse Onassis handed out.

She spent the latter part of her life with Maurice Tempelsman, who was in the diamond business. It isn't the right business to be in if you object to hanging out with mad African dictators who flay the skin off their citizens' backs to get the diamonds that are marketed as precious even though there is no logical reason for any decorative material to be more attractive than any other precious material. Diamonds? Screw it, I'll take cubic zirconia. Jackie never hooked up with clean money (if such a thing exists) like that derived from winemaking or knitting little soft caps for babies. Every male-run fortune Jackie allied herself with was dirty money. If it wasn't bootlegging, it was dodgy oil tankers or blood diamonds. Onassis was a thug. I loved the half-smile she wore at his funeral, not to mention the leather coat. Fashionable, yes, black, yes, but leather!

All these are unpleasant truths, and Jackie ignored them. She had a lot of stuff to ignore—various deaths and scandals in the various families she was linked to—but she had one major thing to ignore. I am not convinced any human has faced this before, but it is part of the modern, filmed world. She frequently had to see her husband get his head blown off via the Zapruder film, with the attendant bits of brain and blood on her face and body and brain matter of such a size that she had to hand a chunk to a doctor in the emergency room of Parkland Hospital.

Imagine that. The Archduke Ferdinand's family probably ran across a few paintings of the event, Princip being the Oswald of his time, but then again, that situation was dwarfed by the slaughter of millions of humans that followed.

Jackie Kennedy coped very well, aside from her chain-smoking, but I do think everyone is allowed one bad habit. Her trick was to ignore. In restaurants she would focus so intently on her guest that the sideways stares of everyone else in the room did not exist for her.

She walled it off.

The problem with Jackie, I imagine, was that she lived in New York, a city she knew by heart so every street corner had its horrible reminder albeit not bits of a husband's cerebellum. All the walled-up stuff she had to ignore—the blood and brain, the press criticism, the slavering public hunger, the studying of every inch of her appearance, the astonishing stupidity of her son as compared to the steadiness and wisdom of her daughter—took up more acreage than other stuff she could easily take in.

Just be thankful your life isn't like that. Whatever happens to you isn't rubbed into your face—Surprise! Assassination on the documentary channel! Watch a spattered Jackie chase Jack's skull fragments!—and your brick wall is intact.

What I'm saying is that you can talk to a therapist and deal with the vile memories. Or you can steadfastly ignore certain events in your life and indeed the continents on which they took place. It's your choice.

I do the latter and it has worked well for me. It has also encouraged a love of travel. Let's go somewhere blank of painful memories! Of course you may build new and even more painful memories on that continent.

But then you can ignore those. Case closed.

Urban versus Rural: Urban Wins

No one knows me here

 One of my childhood
memories is of a windy day somewhere in northern
Canada. I can't say how old I was or where this took place,
as we lived in so many places in the north country. My
mother, who loved rural walks, used to drag me out to God
knows where and we'd stroll for hours. I didn't hate it; I
disliked it, but walking is easy to endure. You just plod.
Eventually you end up back at the car and you go home.
Another glorious afternoon in the scrub pine in the mid-
twentieth-century in the hard-rock Canadian Shield.

It was, as I said, very windy that day. It was howling. The sky was grey, not a depressed grey as in a Toronto sky, or a Tupperware grey as in Vancouver, nor a hard-pavement grey as in London. It was a huge grey. Around us were pine trees, unbeautiful uncharming scrub pines in their millions. Christmas tree shapes? No, scrub pines can't be doing with that nonsense. They just grew up wherever they could get a taste of light and air, scrapey things that would take your skin off if you ran from bears, but so thick that you wouldn't run far.

White pines, with their long soft needles, don't pack themselves in. They drop their needles to make a soft fragrant bed that always makes me think of Arthur Ransome's Swallows and Amazons camping out under the stars. Susan would serve hard-boiled eggs, cocoa and grog. Titty would stare at the stars and imagine things. Good times, those.

This was different. You had scrub pine up to the Arctic Circle and you had gravel roads. That was your choice of landscape. Above you was the harsh sky. Now don't give me that Yorkshire stuff. I bet in Yorkshire they have clouds. The Canadian North can't be bothered with dramatic clouds. It's a flat sky, it is.

And it was windy.

My mother and I both remarked on it. I hate the sound of the wind. Hate it. I only tell you about this one memory because it must offer a clue to the birth of this hatred. Yes, Newfoundland was windy, but so beautiful (it did physically break away from Scotland eons ago) that the wind was very Brontë sisters.

The wind of northern mainland Canada troubled me.

It scared me in a huge subterranean way. Made flesh, that wind was like the hulls of huge ships moving through the water, another sight that scares me so badly that I won't travel by ocean. I can't swim, for one thing. The fate of the American sailors on the U.S.S. *Indianapolis* in 1945 as the crew of the stricken ship was picked off by sharks, one by one, sums up my thoughts on the outer ocean experience.

The best we can hope for is to die in our beds. Being plunked into the ocean with the hull of an ocean liner bearing down on me, that would be the worst.

This is how much the sound of a gale worries me. I love thunder and rain. I hate the lonely moan of the wind. I will lie in my feather bed, books heaped up around me, as I listen to the Sex Pistols or indeed Marvin Gaye, people who sing about pavement anger and sex. And still I can hear this roaring in the background and I am troubled. This is why I love cities.

I chose urban over rural at age seventeen when I was finally able to leave home and go to university. All the school trips I had taken to that point were to cities like Edinburgh or Moscow/Leningrad and Guadalajara. I have never been back into the bush. For you see, in Canada, rural is not the word, really. You have rural hicks, but they live in small towns in southern Ontario. They're just far from things, which is very different from a harsh grey and dusty dark-green landscape that waits to kill you if you venture into it.

I was embarrassed for Werner Herzog when he made a documentary about Tim Treadwell, a silly young man who was devoted to grizzlies and lived on grizzly land in Alaska because urban life hadn't worked out for him. Treadwell was filmed putting his hand on a 10-kilogram load of bear shit, feeling its warmth and saying in his piping Peter Pan voice how wonderful it was to feel the heat of something that had been inside the bear only a moment ago. Inside.

Treadwell ended up inside the bear himself in emphatic fashion shortly after that, but due to the arrival of forest rangers he was not digested. His girlfriend, who clearly was increasingly coming to see that Treadwell was a fool of fantastically irritating proportions, was also eaten although not digested. I don't understand roughing it in the bush. Agoraphobics in my neighbourhood are just as isolated from humans as anyone doing the hermit gig in the dry unvisited hills of Spain. Cities can offer you everything—anonymity, solitude, wild sociability, even that big fish in a small pond thing that makes me laugh with wonder when I see "socialites" pictured in ill-fitting, badly chosen ball gowns in the local [pick your city] money magazines. You can be anybody in a city.

Even after all these years, Jonathan Raban's Soft City, about urban life, has been my schoolbook. It opens with his description of coming out of a kebab-house onto a sidewalk, "head prickly with retsina" and being disoriented. What city is this? But you are you. Whatever city you are in, you are at that moment a stranger to yourself living in a community of strangers. And that is what a city can induce and that is the wonder of it. It's not alienation, Raban says, but something much better. The city is soft. It is waiting for your imprint. You decide what the city will be.

(And there is a side issue here: I stayed too long in the city I moved to when I left the bush. It has become a small town to me. I walk within carefully defined tracks, as though I were a dog peeing on the corners of my habitat. Worse, in those two decades, corporations have flattened urban life so that all cities look the same. They have the same chain stores, the same, admittedly huge, range of food, and evoke the same feelings. This is monstrous. But that is irrelevant. When I was young, I knew every inch of every sidewalk of my small town and they all buzzed with possibility. I have aged in tandem with the power of globalization, and it's my fault too.)

The first time I went to London was with the man I have been in love with for almost all my adult life. We had no money when we started out, which didn't matter, as billionaires would have paid their all for the kind of ecstasy we had then. Everything was new, you see! So we could only travel when he had some work purpose. That first morning he went off to some newspaper office and I ventured out on my own in London. I stood on Oxford Street, just at St. Christopher's Place, taking in the morning sun, the sound of the traffic and the vibrations of the city that came from footsteps and motor cars and breezes in the great parks (breezes, not hard wind, take note), and a feeling of elation and wild freedom came over me such as I had never known before.

It may have been the happiest moment of my life. All this was despite the fact of London's history, that this was the street where De Quincey lost his Ann, that it was near here that Virginia Woolf walked down Bond Street and Regent Street remembering that dinosaurs once trod where these streets led. William Blake's rooms were not far from where I stood. Everything was radiant not just with official history but with personal history, yet I was free to walk here just as Woolf had, taking it all in.

Sarah Don, the jewellery designer and gardener, lives in the country with her husband Monty Don, who was so shattered by the crash of a rather blithe and blind life in the eighties that he is permanently scored with a seasonal depression that will never leave him. He describes what may or may not have been the worst moment. He was sitting in a country hotel for a TV piece he was doing for money, when a heifer walked through the restaurant. It was brown and white, he said, and skittish. Its eyes were scared. The problem was, only he could see a cow in the room. It did not exist. Madness loomed.

Monty Don's books, which describe his horror, have fed me. The only thing that soothes him in the terrible times is working with the soil. He is grounded, he is earthed. But Sarah Don describes in their book *The Jewel Garden* what it meant, during times of intense rat-ridden financial struggle with a rotting husband and three sprightly children, to be able to go to London. The city meant a concentration of energy for her. She needed that injection. She loved the smell of Paddington Station even. She was happiest alone. It refreshed her and gave her a clear head.

I know what she felt. I suspect neither of them likes

people much, after a business failure that lost them their home and any faith in anyone they thought was a friend. Yet Monty gets his comfort from working in the dirt and Sarah gets pumped up by being in a city where she is just as alone.

I feel this elation in most cities I visit, but they have to be foreign and I have to be on my own. I like the knowledge that I will not run into anyone I know. On one of my first trips to Paris, I made great efforts to conceal the fact that I was shattered when a Canadian woman came over to us at a sidewalk café and introduced herself and her husband. They were people we knew or we knew friends of theirs. They were nice. But we avoided those blocks after that and walked around with a hunted feeling. Why do people think I'll recognize them? And even if I did, I am perfectly entitled to snub someone in a foreign city; they're equally eager to snub me.

I told an acquaintance once that I was going to London. So this woman, who I took care never to meet at home, wanted to have lunch with me in in that city. Why? Why, why, why. When she suggested this, I was as tense as if I'd put my jeans on backwards, and I eased myself away, slowly screaming. For she was a rural person passing herself off as an urbanite. Her first instinct in a foreign city was to meet someone from home and be local. She even had the rural look, much like the cow Monty Don saw in the hotel dining room, skittering, its eyes alarmed. What was it doing in a place so foreign to its nature?

Some local writer, very much a Chamber of Commerce type despite his pretensions of being an urbane urbanist, wrote an essay in my local paper about this city, Toronto, being better than Paris because Paris was so deliberately established, so set in its own history, that inhabitants were unable to make a mark on it. Toronto was still a soft city. He could be a star in Toronto, therefore Toronto was better than Paris, which is just about the greatest misreading of Raban anyone could have achieved. The key to the soft city is the anonymity you can achieve. Toronto is new and an inch thick; no one cares about the city and no one cares about you. Paris is what it is; it still doesn't care about you but it is deeply loved by its inhabitants, who are strangers.

I get very angry at people who don't understand the point of urban life. In rural life, all eyes are upon you. This young man was looking for a city where all eyes would be upon him. That is not what most people seek of urbanity. Perhaps he was an American seeking fame. This fame thing, I don't understand it. I cannot imagine anything worse than being famous. What a horror.

As the years pass, it turns out to be just as awful in a different way. In a detached house with the mortgage paid off, I don't have to listen to the artful howls of pleasure from the woman in the apartment next door as she sexes someone. But neighbours are neighbours. Sometimes the distance of a block is not good enough. In my drab yet prissy neighbourhood, I know several young people who were sexually attacked as children—by coaches, babysitters et cetera—and I knew one man who I truly think makes it his life's work. But it was all extremely quiet. Why did I think such crime would be noisy? Douglas

Coupland refers to sex as "fighting crime," and I thought it was witty until I grew old enough to realize that the sex was the crime and there was no fighting it. If I had known what was going on around me, I would have fought. Children needed defending but I didn't know it because I thought all houses were safe houses, especially in a city, and that is why sex criminals rampaging through their own families favour cities.

Maybe cities shouldn't have houses at all. We should all live in terraced houses at best, or in condominiums and apartments, and keep a wandering eye on one another, a drift of attention. The Irish novelist Edna O'Brien says that the problem with rural life is there is no one to hear you scream. But in the polite sections of the city, little girls aren't raised to be screamers. Peel that eye. Watch out. You live in a soft city. Impose yourself upon the place by screaming about the Fred and Rose Wests among us. Take notice of the child turned suddenly silent. Ask questions. It's a city. There's no need to be polite. You can up sticks any time you wish.

It's a myth I've built in my own mind that I have to stay in this city I know too well now. I could pack my tent and steal away in the night to find another soft city in which to hide.

Born Ugly

In which we humans dodge a painful truth

 I was struck by a blind-
ing insight this week, a blindingly unpleasant insight,
and when I say struck, I do mean with a dead snake.

My girlfriend M— once killed a rattler at her cottage, and since the rule is that you're supposed to take the
corpses to the nearest Forest Ranger Bob for statistical
purposes, she bagged the snake and put it in the trunk of
her junky cottage car. And forgot about it for two whole
months. That was the state of the snake chunks that hit
me in the face. The bearer of foul tidings was *The Observer,*

a British Sunday paper owned by the same people who put out *The Guardian*. In an attempt to win new readers in a flashy tabloid world, they shrank the paper, went full-colour and decided to put out a weekly thing called *Observer Woman*. Excellent, I thought. A fine thoughtful magazine from which I shall crib all my column ideas! Pay levels, the struggles and pleasures of Third World Women, ethical shopping, and the electroshock that hits a young university-educated woman when she enters her first workplace. So far, *Observer Woman* has told me about body hair (naked woman in stilettos with one hirsute, insulation-quality leg), about fashion (headline: "Mmm, nice bit of skirt. But are you a tulip or a pencil?"), health (naked woman squashed as though she were about to be put into a suitcase to illustrate an article on irregular periods), a new feminist who poses naked with a fig leaf to make feminism attractive to women (or is it men?) celebrity housewives like Jerry Hall and Trudy Styler posed like statuary, long frozen stalks in toile de Jouy ballgowns in front of their gloss-painted London homes. You know the drill.

We women can cope with magazines like this, mainly because we have to. That's all there is. The fact that you'd expect much much more of *The Observer*, is, well, it's just bloody typical.

But this week, the cover was a wrinkle-free eighteen-year-old with perfect infant skin encased in headband and dark glasses and bound by Band-Aids. Yes, it was "How Do I Look? Confessions of a Botox Convert." But it was written by an intelligent feature writer whose articles

I can generally count on to be good. She's someone to be taken seriously. I trust her. She entertains me. She does everything a good journalist is supposed to do.

Change all that to past tense.

For she, disgracing everything she has ever believed, had herself injected with Botox, had unseemly skin patches lasered away and the rest of her skin treated with Retin-A. She was also given cleanser, sunscreen and eye cream (and it must be said that these last three were new to her, so fair enough).

We are shown three honest shadowless white-light photos, before Botox, five days after, and ten days after. And she looks worse in each picture. Which isn't even the point, but we'll get to that.

She looks dreadful. She has been dragged through a hedge backwards three times, she is coated in Botox snake venom, her hair is filthy, she has pores you could dip a soup ladle into, and she has a lard-pie face. That means a big piece of splodge that spills over at the edges because she is a big comfy fatty woman. She's an over-stuffed sofa of a human, and yet this doesn't save her face, as they tell you. (Skinny bodies mean clawlike faces; well-upholstered bodies mean fat, unwrinkled faces. Once you hit fifty, choose one or the other.)

I show the pictures to my husband and ask him how old he thinks she is. After the customary bickering, he hunkers down, studies the three photos and says "Oh, fifty." Which is what I thought as well.

She is thirty-six.

And he's right. She looks fifty in every photograph.

Evangelical Christians preface their conversations with "Have you heard the good news?" (It's not the news you expect, which is why they irritate people.) Have you heard the bad news? It isn't dieting or buying expensive unguents or even a professional makeup application (though the bored cosmeticians always consult the 6-foot, 7-inch bony green-haired black man, mid–skin bleach, who's running the show, and then gives you purple lips, in my experience) that makes a woman look good. It's being born good-looking that does it.

Look at this poor woman, noodged into this by a pushy editor who loves it when female journalists can be suckered into poisoning themselves. She is homely. Fact. She must have been born that way or she wouldn't be looking so haunted and awful by magazine standards, and so utterly average by human standards.

In the first photograph, she looks like someone trying to stay brave after the death of her father, which in fact she was.

In the second, she has just been told that her life sentence in a Bangkok jail for being caught with a coke balloon up her arse at Passport Control has been commuted to 39.5 years.

In the third, she looks wary, pale as bleached canvas, as you do in a mug shot while you're trying to tell the police officer it was all a horrid misunderstanding. You thought you ran over a cat. Turns out it was a human grandma.

And when she is loaded with makeup, shoved into zebra-striped sandals, fishnet stockings, a gauzy grey dress that conceals her bulky contours, and is finally

made to wash her hair and grin manically, she looks
tragic. The be-suited dermatologist who's behind all this
lolls on a modernist white plastic chair (not his fault;
those chairs are positively dental in their recline) staring
at her bemusedly, frowning. It is the male gaze and it is
troubling.

I love you, journalist woman, I say. I love everyone
who's unknowingly being humped by a real pack of grossly
overpaid pretentionists. You're a good writer and a good
person. I will continue to enjoy your writing and your
clever mind. It doesn't matter that you were intimidated
into letting a payer of fees urge you into this public strip-
ping. Oh, and is it a coincidence that now you write a column saying you no longer think the statue in Trafalgar
Square of the armless, legless artist Alison Lapper is a
great work of art? You're more interested in conventional
beauty now.

But back to the bigger problem.

When was the last time you saw a truly stunningly
beautiful person? Or even a strikingly attractive one?
Those women can walk around wearing anything, without
makeup, and their smile is like a light bulb for their face.
I know. I've seen about two of them.

We humans are not beautiful. Or else we are, so we
developed impossible standards for beauty just to make
life more spiky and difficult. What the woman journalist's
sad article reveals is that only those born beautiful can be
genuinely beautiful. For the rest of us, it is not going to
happen. I think we should just aim for hygiene, a scalp
not layered with sebum, an ear not sprouting sticky hair.

One honest plastic surgeon told the journalist that the first thousand pounds should go on a good haircut and a makeup session. He's right.

There's really nothing that can be done if you aren't born with that magic mix on your face that equals beauty. Intelligence and wit enhances it. Good bones really do matter. In fact, good bones can do it all. You'll be interestingly gorgeous at eighty.

But women have been trained not to want that. They've been trained to want artificial beauty. They cannot have it.

I never wanted it, and I can't quite understand the reason. Perhaps I knew it was impossible. I do groom myself excessively. It's work, work, work, talk about your Magdalen Laundries, just washing, exfoliating, moisturizing, facializing, cutting, conditioning, self-tanning, removing hair, filing, ridge-filling, painting/lining/blending and spending countless thousands on a fine wardrobe appropriate to my own odd little body of which I am fond.

But when, in my early twenties, I saw a plastic surgeon about a deviated septum that was causing me to breathe out of just one nostril, he said, "I'm not supposed to say this to patients, but do you want your nose fixed while I'm in there?" I did not. I have a prominent hooked nose. But I knew even then that I wasn't going to be beautiful. I was aiming more for interesting, because that might be achievable. It had been achievable thus far.

He ran the burns unit. I always imagined him caring for third-degree burns patients, crusted and weeping salt tears that worsened the pain, knowing they would be forever hideous if they lived. Did he not rather despise silly people like me with my little breathing problem, as he arrived an hour late after treating a freshly barbecued patient, to pull what looked like 20 metres of bloody gauze out of my left nostril like a clown hauling endless handkerchiefs from his sleeve?

I had thought he might, but I changed my mind in the recovery room where a young woman had had her breasts enlarged at his hands. "Are you in pain?" he asked her. "Remember, you have to suffer pain for beauty."

But you don't, Doctor. You have to be born with beauty. What's more, with the kind of beauty that will last: a strong jaw, good cheekbones, interesting eyes that are never vacant of interest or knowledge, a face that radiates strength and kindness.

The woman writer has snake poison in her face now. Where do women draw the line at what can enter through a needle? Offal? The bane of the pork industry, the pale reddish "exudate" that leaks from mushy pig meat? The sweat of a jogging George Clooney or a huntin' Dick Cheney, free-flowing and slightly yellowed? I wouldn't want to kiss a face full of that.

She says the frown groove between her eyebrows is gone, but despite rumours, she can still frown although the lines are scant. So why struggle to frown? It's not as though the salesperson who sold you the wrong ink cartridge for your printer is going to notice or care. So she will now have to rely on her eloquence the next time her editor asks her to invite a million people to laugh at her.

She won't be able to do what I do: frown, lift one eyebrow and slant the lip so as to create a full-face sneer that remains dignified yet dismissive to a perfect chisel-end of contempt.

I remember once sitting in the office of a newspaper editor I normally got along with. I was furious. I bubbled and seethed, I popped and frothed. Eventually he extracted the problem from between my locked teeth; it was not fair that the designer of my page, a really talented woman, was being paid less than someone brought in from outside.

You're one of those people who can radiate intense feeling from your face and body without saying a word, he said calmly. It's rare.

It's useful to be able to do that. It gets you ten grand in salary that a merely pretty face wouldn't get you. The journalist began her article describing her face in the morning. Every part of her face sags. Her mouth is turned down.

Didn't anyone tell her the Nancy Mitford secret from *Love in a Cold Climate?* Before entering a room, say the word "brush." One will appear before the crowd with a mouth that looks as one would wish.

There is no need for snaky liquids.

You are not beautiful. Almost no one is. We start with the race already halfway run and then we age to boot, so get used to it.

Try to be interesting, and work on the content of your character, not the pallor of your skin. Oh, and wash your hair.

The Triangle of Death

Every garden has one

 There's a corner of my garden where things go to die. No, that's not right. Plants spread but they don't actually travel. What I mean is that when I prepare the soil—a huge hole with compost, top-soil and some peat, properly mixed—and place the plant in it, it dies, sometimes within weeks or even days.

(Don't worry; this isn't an essay about gardening.)

Now I know that plants placed up against a stone wall live in dry grey conditions that cause death. And one side of the death triangle is indeed a stone wall. I amend that soil. I water with care and attention. So it's not that. Few plants can cope with the speckled shade of that corner. It has a lilac tree hanging over it that also conceals the detritus of the neighbour behind us, as well as the orange plastic sheeting that covers his trucks in all seasons.

I choose plants that prefer almost total darkness. Still, they turn yellow, limp, brown, sometimes blackish. Even hardy shrubs like weigela, and euonymus for fuckety's sake, get skint and thin. They turn pale. They fail to thrive, like the children of overly attentive parents.

How does a pine tree die? Right now, I've shaved the trunk of every protruding failed stick. On top there's a sort of shag bit. I give the thing a bucket of water a day in a hollowed-out circle around its central stick—you can hardly call it a trunk—and after ten years, the thing is, oh, five feet high.

What survives in that corner is a brushed steel obelisk and a huge round Dutch-blue ceramic pot that is, needless to say, empty. For this corner is not for the living. Were it not for my hatred of tweeness, I'd shove more dead objects in there—a little red wagon, a stuffed meerkat, anything at all that can't die because it's already dead.

You can see the metaphor coming, can't you. The death triangle, easily visible from my bedroom window, is the corner of the garden on which I lavish the most care and worry. It was only when I gave up on the fern corner that it began to flourish and now the borders are filling in with a lavishness not commensurate with the care I took with them. I don't believe in harsh pruning, as S. does, and the garden is dotted with a circle of little green sticks that he feels certain are about to explode into foliage. I remain calm. Foliage will not there be. If you're going to nurture false hopes, why don't you stick with the non-flowering peony, now aged seven, or the trumpet vine that has never squawked, much less trumpeted. As for the honeysuckle, it's just a green thing that snakes up the pergola for no purpose that I can see. I have grown to love twining it around itself.

S. sneers. No flowers, he says. Yes, I say, but it has foliage. All I ask of a plant is a little greeny bit.

The fact is that life on this planet has been so sour for years now that I have lost my sense of humour. I gaze out my window at my marvellous corner collection of failures and it seems appropriate somehow. For I have stopped trying. I just order blinds online from Ikea, which the website informs me will result in confirmation within twenty-four hours. It doesn't, of course. When I call them, I realize that the blinds Ikea has decided to offer me are not the size I ordered, which is moot since they are not available online. But they are, I protest. I clicked on the bit that said "only view items available online." There were two items. I chose one.

That's why we confirm. We're changing our site and those blinds are not for sale.

So Ikea failed to call me, to register the correct size and to tell the truth on its website. That's three failures for one little $12 window blind that I only bought online so I wouldn't have to go into one of their dreadful stores where things are no longer "out of stock" but "oversold," which makes it the customer's fault.

Ikea is like my Triangle of Death. Nothing grows there, nothing flourishes.

What you do with Triangles of Death is, I think, pave them. Give up. It's only this year that I realized, all by my lonesome, that it was possible to give up, that there was no shame in doing so, and that in fact it was often the only sensible course. Drop that thang. Let it go. There comes a point when you cease to care. It is no longer a defeat but an amusing fact one can scarcely bring oneself to dwell on. It recedes startlingly quickly, contradicting every claim one's parents ever made about stick-to-it-iveness and grim determination. Quit.

S. and I used to debate this. The plant would be so dead its blackened leaves would emit an actual odour. Of rotting. And he'd be saying, Not dead yet! We used to exchange this role over the years, back and forth.

And then I had this editor. She was so awful I learned to laugh at her. I didn't want to complain about her. She was such good copy, you see. And S. said one day, I think you'll have to leave. You can't tolerate this treatment.

Sure I can, I said. She's giving me great quotes. Not dead yet!

How did this happen? To this day, I am the great thrower-outer. Few things give me more pleasure than disposal. I'm hoping as you read this that McDonald's, well, sit 'n' shits, you can hardly call them restaurants, will be receding from the landscape. To my mind, the worst thing about Happy Meals is not the grotesque McFood but the plastic toys they hand out to greedy, chemically dazed children. We had crates of these things.

I used to wait for a garbage day when I was alone at home and quietly turf them. Even the most acquisitive of children can't keep track of McDonald's' crapulent little figures derived from fossil fuel, dye and Chinese fingers. They live in landfill now and will for hundreds of years after I am gone. Not dead yet!

But they are out of sight.

Therapists seem so magical. You tell them your problems, desperately hunting for a solution. And the therapist suggests quite calmly that perhaps there isn't one. Your husband will always be this way. Your mother is too old to change. Your siblings are odd and will become odder. This plant has been dead for years. Put a rock in that spot or an obelisk, something inert.

There are Chinese women, newly wealthy, who want to be taller and actually undergo surgery to lengthen their legs. You can imagine what that entails: breaking the bones, inserting a whole new metal crankshaft and lying on a bed of pain for months until you can hobble about with no one except other shortish Chinese even noticing. And they're noticing the limp, not your extra 6 centimetres.

There's an actress I adore, Kristin Scott Thomas or Resse Witherspoon or someone. She's 5 foot 3 inches. And why shouldn't she be? She's magnificent. She radiates such life force that no one suggests she shatter her shins and assemble something totteringly taller. That plant is dead. Enjoy the statuary corner. It faces facts, it does.

Easily the greatest insight I was handed about abstract art was that it was all landscapes. So now I look at the landscape and see the dead zone and the ferny territory and the tangled place in transition and it all works somehow. We don't give up on enough things. Republicans, neocons, Bushes, most Americans, magical realism, Swedish efficiency, British cleanliness, Philip Roth, arrogant young white males, people and their failed hair— just give up on it, they're finished, they're over. Abandon hope.

I greatly enjoyed my youth when everything, and I mean the totality of what crossed or could possibly eventually cross my path, was of interest to me. But it's over. Place it in the Triangle of Death, the place where things go to dry up and become stationary. This is as it should be.

It is a necessary zone. The gnawed bones of the 1973 victims of the Andes crash who were eaten by their starving fellow passengers were buried in one grave, piled with as many rocks as the clean-up crew could muster, and marked with an iron cross. Even then, that grave's no match for an avalanche or a rock slide or a glacial melt caused by climate change.

Say goodbye. It is polite and sensible. It is reasonable. It is good.

An Open Letter to My Writer's Block

What did I ever do to you?

Yes, I stole this idea from that section in *McSweeney's* which I never read because I'm too busy not writing this book. I was primed not to like *McSweeney's*, but those open letters to people or things that are unlikely to respond are pretty funny. I'll go read some more of them now.

Yes, the letters to Louis XIV and to the birds nesting in people's air conditioners are hilarious while poignant, and this letter isn't going to be either of those things. But I feel strong emotions coming on and I don't appear to be able to drink enough cold white wine to even start the original essay, which was supposed to be about the U.S. House of Representatives who disgrace the very idea of white men, or to bindweed which I can't exterminate in my front garden by hand (back garden, yes, because nobody's watching me) because it's too weird.

It's not as weird as standing beside the brick exterior of my house and picking off the little five-pointed dried white suckers that used to attach the Virginia creeper that ebbs and flows on the walls as the decades pass. You see, dear Writer's Block, this is what I'm reduced to doing after hours in my office trying to find the inspiration, the sheer drive, that old sense of humour that used to swing my hips and set my fingers a-typing, anything that would make the river flow. I really used to write like that before I met you, WB. I had the passion. I had that pleasure gland that made me want to win the reader over with that concise yet stippled effect that worked for, well, some people. But you took that away from me.

What am I going to tell Knopf, WB? I used to laugh at word counts, knowing I'd only surpass them, and tell even untrustworthy editors to hack away. I always had more columns in there somewhere, and always too long. But do you know what you have made me into, WB? You have turned me into a Russell Hokes.

You know that name. It's famous in Blocked circles. Also known as Amy Sedaris–Paul Dinello–Stephen Colbert who wrote the novel *Wigfield: The Can-Do Town That Just May Not,* Hokes was the fictional writer contracted to write a book about America's vanishing small towns. Woefully unqualified to write even a letter of complaint to his cable dealer, Russell Hokes hit upon Wigfield, a town about to have its dam demolished (even though it had no river to block and thereby flood the place, thus destroying the town and making the citizens eligible for huge federal grants). The entire book, consisting of transcribed interviews with the town's three mayors, strippers, and plastic surgeons operating out of trailers next to the Tit Time, was written with 50,000 things in mind.

They were words, WB. How I laughed when I first read *Wigfield*, written by a man who lived in terror that he couldn't come up with the fifty grand needed to earn his advance. Books by Folks Whut Cant Rite. It was funny then, WB.

It's not funny now. Something happened. I need another 10,000 to 20,000 words. You took them from me, Writer's Block. All I think about now is how you managed it. How did you turn someone who thought of writing as finger exercise, someone who typed while her "A Dozen Rosas" or even "Buy-Buy Tokyo" nails (OPI nail polish) were still drying, could end up sitting in front of a computer for six hours and not think of a single thing to say, how did you do this to me, WB? I'm Russell Hokes, stealing articles from the *Wigfield Sporadic* to up his word count.

Look, I've had therapy. She was great. But she can't crack the writer's block. She doesn't even say what a cowardly therapist would say: "Only you can understand your writer's block." No, she tries. I mean, she tried. I could kill you, WB.

Is it self-esteem? Do I hate myself? No. I think I'm rather nice, actually. I'm kind to children. The mistreatment of other people drives me to rage and I don't just seethe, I take action. I'm tidy, I have a nice wardrobe and I wear makeup even on days when I don't go out. I donate to Amnesty International and subscribe to union-run feminist magazines. I even send money to reptile shelters and I hate snakes. Apparently they're part of the bug-eating cycle and we need that or something. I vote for the underdog even when I suspect that my income nudges me into the overdog area and not just because I used to be something of an underdog myself (but I was only poor because I was living off my parents) but because it's right. I watch out for tiny abandoned children in malls just to stay level with the child molesters and, look, basically I am okay.

Is it that I suspect the manuscript I am due to hand in in twenty-two days, a month past deadline—and I have never missed a deadline in my life, WB—is a mess? No, because my editor is smart and I can fix the mess lickety-split as long as I have 65,000 words to goddamn rearrange. I was raised a girl. I aim to please. That's not the problem.

Does it have something to do with having written a political column for eighteen months, worse, a syndicated column that runs around the world (I picture it in jogging gear, all sweaty and disgusting) in many languages? I have to censor myself in this column because no wisecrack survives seven languages, yes. I worry about offending my U.S. editor with my constant spew over George W. Bush and his fractured mind. I can't say what I really think about the Dutch turning racist because maybe I'm published there. There are some countries they mention on my royalty statement that I can't identify. They may be Baltic.

Okay, that might be a brake on free-range writing. But it's political commentary and that's not what this book is about. So you have another weapon, don't you, WB, something that goes way deeper under the skin?

I read about this parrot in a David Sedaris essay. Sedaris's sister, Lisa, was in college and she trained her parrot to shout out encouraging messages. "You can do it, Lisa!" the parrot would croak. So I told S. to say in happy talk, "Go Heather!" and "Just do it!" (that was the Nike slogan that Naomi Wolf—to her credit, she was ashamed— used in her *Fire with Fire* feminist book). But S. is British and he couldn't bark these phrases at me without cracking up. And this enraged me, so I said, You go write a book then, and I felt bad because he doesn't want to write a book and also that is stupid to say because I don't want to write a book any more either. And now he is downstairs watching the World Cup final, and I am up here typing about not typing.

Coffee doesn't work on me. Exercise energizes me, but only to paint drywall. Writing doesn't require physical energy, it requires a chair and an ass to put on it and maybe a commitment. A commitment that ran faster than me.

The truth is, I didn't expect George Bush to be re-elected in 2004. I just didn't think a developed nation could be that dumb. And even if the election was stolen, and I'm certain, along with Robert F. Kennedy, Jr., that it was, it wasn't stolen by that much, which means there is a huge mass of terminally dumb and cruel people who have isolated fine smart Democratic voters who will spend the next few years slowly cracking up like the crackle surface of a vase instead of getting their act together and moving up to Canada.

And I guess I couldn't take it. The only thing that kept me going through 2004 was Jon Stewart, and after that Stephen Colbert, but I don't know, at some point, I stopped laughing. I had other allies. Kurt Vonnegut wrote a book. Springsteen did his Seeger album. John Tulloch, a victim of the Tube bombings in London, wrote of his continued devotion to free-speechers like Harold Pinter and Ken Loach even though his injuries have left him with vertigo so severe he can't even get into a cab. Even former conservatives started backtracking. But Betty Friedan, Susan Sontag, John Kenneth Galbraith and Hunter S. Thompson died. That left Noam Chomsky and he's getting on.

I know, the Brits laughed all through the Second World War, but look at them now with their Tony Blair, the joke's on them. And then Canada handed a minority government to a goober with a flabby belly and wet lips, a touch of Asperger's, and a wardrobe from Canadian Tire. He killed national day care and blew billions on the military—what is the point of Canada having a military? We're so land-big that we're like moose; we just stand there and get shot, it's not like we're gonna fight back— and I had always ignored Canadian politics and I suddenly realized I had a new burden.

All the Western nations were turning shithead. Sure,

Latin and South America, they were getting their act together, but basically I had nowhere to go. There were riots in Paris and, yes, the French students were splendid, but face it, the French treat their immigrants like field slaves.

And at some point, I couldn't laugh, so I couldn't write. Most of the comedy was about sex and drugs and that was no help. Sex and drugs are things you do; the comedy is an add-on. All Hollywood movies were SFX blockbusters; when Americans made a movie they thought was serious it was *Sideways* or *The Squid and the Whale*, films about repellent people who should be taken outside and shot, or maybe just shot. I felt like Catherine O'Hara, who said after she watched *Sex, Lies and Videotape*, "Who are these people?"

I marched about the house pointlessly after that *Squid* movie. I swear, I could have become a social conservative after seeing divorcing parents behave that way in front of their children. KIDS DON'T WANT TO HEAR ABOUT YOUR MAN AND LADY BITS, GOT THAT? And I've never met a book person like that father played by Jeff Daniels. If they're really like that—and, yes, there is one asshole in every book club like that but that is a law of book clubs—then maybe books should be burned.

See, those movies, about wine, and books, and sex, were intended to be comedies. WB, is that how you did it? Because I found them so repulsive, so unfunny, that I wanted to knit myself a balaclava (one with no holes, naturally) and sit in a closet after seeing it. If people are really like that, I give up.

And obviously, if they are like that they're not going to like this book beyond the fact that the writer is sliding into a horrific depression that makes her unable to write a book that sane people like.

But there didn't seem to be any sane people around, is my point. Was this your plan, WB, or am I crediting you with powers you don't possess? People haven't changed surely; it's only voting patterns, circumstances and my own view of things that have changed.

So there I stood, literally picking at my house. That Virginia creeper leaves a million little dry stalks and suckers on the brick. I could spend the rest of my life picking at it, and I started to. It was restful.

I found I could no longer read fiction. Yes, of course I could still read Munro and Atwood and Lessing. The best fiction will survive anything. But fiction was sliding downhill fast and naturally, WB, you directed that I would be particularly bereft, you little shit.

So I turned to non-fiction. This is the age of the memoir and the splendid history; we are at our peak. The problem from my point of view was that people were telling the truth, the awful truth, and failing to cover pain with jokes. This would be admirable under normal circumstances, but with WB, I had nothing to say. It was not my aim to depress people.

I really take it as significant that this was when I began to boycott things in earnest—American chain stores with their goods produced by perfect saffron hands for twelve cents an hour, foods flown across the planet at what cost to climate change, gardening shoppes because

I was sick of twee crap, The Body Shop after it was bought by L'Oréal which is part-owned by evil Nestlé even though I still buy their mascara and am not sure whether they own Lancôme which dropped Isabella Rossellini as a model because she was too old and we could go on in this vein forever. I, who used to buy like a down-market version of Nicole in Fitzgerald's *Tender Is the Night,* had stopped shopping.

This was not normal. This was not good. It meant that I had given up on one of the big ingredients in sensuality—beautiful clothes and things that smelled good.

Was this a tactic, WB, or a result? Because what's better than good words? Those are sensual too.

But that's too simple, WB. I was depressed so I couldn't write? It never stopped me before, you sly boots. I've been depressed my entire life—what sane person isn't—but it had never before stopped the shower of words words words words.

Not only did you stop my words, you stopped me liking other people's words and for that I will pull out your soft liver and feed it to the squirrels who infest my garden, I notice. They really are nasty, quick, sneaky rodents, just like you, WB.

We have our tactics, though. There's no end of the line for me, you know. Because, WB, I still loved my Virginia Woolf. I have always thought that whatever happened, I could crawl into bed with my Virginia and read her for years, as I used to for years when I was young and didn't have to read or write for money. Larry McMurtry, author of the great novel *Lonesome Dove,* who can no longer write because of the depression that resulted from the fact of his open-heart surgery—the human core sometimes cannot stand being maintained by a machine that does the pumping and breathing; awful things result—called her the Blue Nile of writing.

You couldn't steal that, you ill-read cheap-arsed comic-licking Game Boy WB, could you.

Words words words. Use your words, they tell little children who hit. Unfortunately that's all I have for you, WB. Once I figure it out, your tactic, how you did this to me after years of me watching and learning and using my words, I'll crush you.

You have my word on that, you hateful skin-digger, you virus, you whip-limbed jelly mutator. You will pay.

How You Americans Annoy Me

And how I wish you would just stop

It's almost too easy to write this; I imagine it's an assigned essay in every English class in the world (they no longer do How I Spent My Summer Vacation). But it feels marvellous to vent, to spew, to exude, to expel my utter contempt for that old circus elephant down south.

I don't understand why I should be expected *not* to like or dislike Americans or why "anti-American" is seen as an epithet in some circles. The United States at its best is annoying; at its worst it is fatal to one's health. When I meet someone who isn't anti-American, and I include Americans in this, I think they're either stupid or they've been busy with eighteen-month-old twins and haven't had the time to think about it.

Note: When I say "Americans," I mean the awful ones, and 99 percent of the time we're talkin' Red State. Or neocons who live in Blue States while Bush is in power.

Let's get started, friends. I am reading the U.S. men's magazine *The New Yorker,* to which I subscribed when Seymour M. Hersh was first using its pages to break news stories about the catastrophe that is the war in Iraq. Of course as soon as I subscribed, he stopped writing for them. This always happens to me. (An aside: Just as you can't take a marriage for granted, never count on the excellence of a newspaper, a magazine, a writer or a TV show. They waver in quality as editors move about, good writers leave and redesigns leave the thing unrecognizable. I'd cancel *The New Yorker* but I can't be bothered.)

Their writer Adam Gopnik disappointed me when he referred to British MP George Galloway's fiery appearance before a Senate committee as "bizarre." Galloway, a Scot, was objecting to being libelled by a senator, minute in brain and stature, over humanitarian donations to Iraq. He spoke with biblical eloquence and with the fire of William Wallace. Every sentence that emerged from his mouth was like an angel by Bernini, perfectly formed, firmly placed. Gopnik, who had been back in New York for some time, had become an American again. He had lost his sense of humour and his appreciation of publicly displayed intellect as well as the love of personality that imbues many European parliamentarians, even in their current soggy state.

It was sad to lose Adam.

Then Jeffrey Toobin, who did admirable work covering the trial of Orenthal Simpson as well as the Clinton impeachment, wrote a piece on the World Cup aptly titled "Un-American Activity." He wrote, "Soccer is the Canada of American sports, viewed less with contempt than indifference." (He then went on to interview the war criminal Henry Kissinger on his thoughts on the World Cup, as extraordinary a lapse in taste as I have ever read. Why not call Albert Speer about the new glassiness of Berlin architecture? Would slave labour do it better, Al?) Americans are notoriously clump-headed when it comes to other countries, but surely they can grasp their own natures? No? Americans don't like soccer because they haven't yet triumphed at it. But they love their absurdly named World Series because, by definition, it's next to impossible for an American not to win it.

The fact is, Americans would have loved to have defeated Ghana. It must have hurt bad to be defeated by the sleek, elegant forms of soccer players from a poverty-stricken African nation. They didn't even realize that it was a compliment to be defeated by Ghana, which was only knocked out of the Cup early because it had the misfortune to be up next against Brazil.

Americans really do believe winning is the only thing. This makes them want to win at any cost, which is why the world cringes when they show up at the Ryder

Cup with the players' wives in matching linen sheath dresses, and why the American crowds heckle foreign players. They win at any cost, and that means badly. Worse, they sulk in defeat. For they hold every other nation in contempt, even as their empire disintegrates. Yes, it is rather fun to watch (until you see Iraqi bodies pile up), because they don't understand the contempt in which *they* are held. The rest of the world would love to get genuine indifference from the United States. Instead they get belligerence. Every fight must be a fight to the death.

It's the same stance that makes the U.S. consumer demand that every purchase must be made at the lowest possible cost. Cheap goods are a win. But Americans are incapable of following the clues dropped along the logic trail. Cheap goods are generally shoddy and their popularity is responsible for the—it's not a rash so much as a deep-burrowing flesh-eating disease—omnipresence of white plastic objects across that nation. There isn't anything Americans don't like in vinyl, and that includes white picket fences, "wicker" furniture, above-ground swimming pools, buildings, shoes, and the list goes on.

These goods are made in China. Why Americans should then allow themselves to be told that Mexicans are stealing their jobs, when clearly they are giving away those jobs to the American hunger for cheap Chinese crap . . . it's a mystery. No, it's not.

Americans are dumb.

There, I've said it.

They're nice people, many of them in the Blue States, but they don't read, their insularity practically turns them inside out, they dress like children and they're so literal-minded that even Americans can't understand how their intelligent comedy survives. The audience is so tiny. Their novelists are so pompous they explode in a flinging of beard stubble while failing to understand that a huge canvas of American crassness is out there waiting, begging, to be painted. But no, they'd rather study their own tortured souls. Their magazines are humourless and their carnal urges are for women who look like little girls.

Infantilism is the American watchword. Chemical dermabrasion is just another term for facial skin like a baby's bottom. Americans like big eyes, pulpy pink lips and pug noses. Baby faces. (Actually, the pulpy pink lips might be ascribed to something else entirely.) They like youth, even in the non-young, which has led to evil things.

Oh, the gasps that come from normal people catching a glimpse of John Travolta, Michael Douglas, Kenny Rogers or Barry Manilow after losing sight of them for twenty years. What the hell did he do with his head? These people's old faces are now sitting on top of their heads; their faces are a tight, trim stripe of neck skin. People like Linda Tripp and Katherine Harris have entire head transplants. With breast implants, what you have is small children with beach balls in their chests, covered with human skin.

American grown-ups wear overalls, T-shirts, sneakers and white ankle socks with their Keds. I saw a reporter show up for an interview on *The Colbert Report* about his book on the U.S. hostage crisis (something about it being the start of the continuing Islamic war on the United States) in a lime-green short-sleeved sports shirt and sandals. Sandals on a grown man. On TV. In the evening.

Americans have a limited range of references and will never catch yours, which means they don't get jokes. They have no shared literacy, which means that intelligent books are impossible to market. You're looking for five people in every city and maybe they're busy that day.

Oh, and their food. Huge portions, all fried, all glistening with fat and coated with something cheesy. The one thing Americans got right, sportswear, has become impossible because of the growth of the American ass on this fatty, aorta-blocker of a menu. You cannot look elegantly casual while fat. The lines aren't there, only the bulges they don't even put in kids' cartoons any more. And even when an American gets thin, it's not because he said no to enormous portions of disgusting filler-food, it's because he had his stomach stapled into something the size of an ankle sock and now he can only eat one potato chip on the hour. An American person is a hog. If he were sliced up, his meat would be pale and tasteless, like a modern pork chop. Things are so bloaty that to combat childhood obesity, American thinkers have suggested making toys heavy. I am not making this up. Rather than sending children out to play or stopping them from stuffing their cake-holes at McDonald's, they're considering putting weights in stuffed toys and building blocks. Playtime as workout. What they haven't considered is the nature of children. Someone's going to lose an eye.

Anyway, and I thought of this first, Americans should

have huge iron cutlery, so heavy it takes two hands to lift it. Not only would they exercise while eating but they wouldn't be able to eat those huge portions. Good idea or what?

Americans never stop eating. In fact, they never stop anything, never do one thing at a time. They're always multi-tasking. In other countries, this means talking on a cell phone while walking or driving. Since Americans don't walk, they talk in their cars while eating, usually food-on-a-stick, and by the way, they have no notion of when to stop when it comes to devising stuff on a stick. They sell meat popsicles that you can force up from the bottom of the cup, and don't tell me that isn't worse than Twizzlers. It's mystery meat. The only buzz comes from seeing how oddly food can be designed so as to be conveniently adjacent to the American mouth.

Americans choose not to think. No, that's wrong. It's not a choice. The capacity isn't there. I read BBC Online's report on the Bush Administration threatening *The New York Times* for reporting that the government is secretly studying the bank accounts of American citizens. It includes comments from readers. And there he is, the typical American, John of New York telling the world, "If your transactions are completely legitimate, then why should you be worried?" John, if your colon is completely empty, then why should you object to a search of your anal cavity?

Here's what one of my favourite humans, Mil Millington, who wrote the brilliant novel called *Things My Girlfriend And I Have Argued About,* has to say on his Web mail about American brain function: "Even my limited experience suggests most Americans are extremely pleasant people. I'm just sorry that the majority have to share a country with such a large minority of yawping, jingoistic, humourless, moronic wankers. Oh, and my sympathies about your President too."

He adds, "Let me repeat what I just said there so there can be no possible mistake. We have, dear people of the Internet, a hard core of morons. They are: dull-eyed, humourless (though they think they aren't), wearisome, insistently vocal and—consistently—American. However, how-ev-er, the large majority of Americans are quite, quite lovely. I adore them all. If one of my children ever came home and said, 'Father, I'm in love with an American,' I'd swell with delight. I'd have a feast prepared and bells rung. Americans are ace. I genuinely do like Americans. Excluding (for obvious reasons) the French, then the only set of people I think are more rubbish than not are the English—sullen, littering drunks, clutching a mobile phone in one hand while in the other there is a lead which ends in a crapping dog. OK? Is that plain? America—come here, I want to kiss each and every one of your pretty faces. Tch."

Back to me. Americans can't grasp principles or ideas, only things. I keep a gun beside my bed, an American will say. The gun is then stolen and used to kill a child. Not his fault, the American says. Because guns don't kill people, people kill people. The fact that the gun is a wildly effective way to kill people, much better than bare hands, is not mentioned. They use those guns to rampage through the world, killing millions of people who are, not by coincidence, smaller and more beautiful than Americans.

Millions of children starve because Americans swelled up on this planet and nothing can be done.

Yet Americans at home are so obedient. Their Congress hasn't raised the minimum wage since 1997. It stands at $5.15 an hour. But they did vote to reduce the estate tax, so that only the top half of a percent of estates will pay it. This will cost the government $602 billion over the next ten years, money it sorely needs from people who don't need it at all. But this is just fine with Americans because they think that one day they will be in that top half of a percentage of the money pyramid. They have no clue that they will probably die in harness while still young, all the while saying, Thank yuh, thank yuh, land of opportunity. It's hard not to despise people that dumb, admit it. Your children will likely be poorer than you, you tell them. Thank yuh, thank yuh, land of opportunity.

My God, what a place. We used to call them slow learners, and then we called it special ed, but half the country is so stupid you wouldn't tolerate it in a six-year-old. That's why they're racist. Stupid people always have to feel better than someone else. So the whites dump on the blacks, probably because the blacks are better-looking. I can't think of any other reason to envy black people in the U.S.A. Americans tie black men to the backs of their trucks and drag them down back roads in Texas until they disintegrate, and you like that, don't you. Their women wear blue eyeshadow and *Be-lie-eve* in songs by Cher. Don't deny it.

And all these stupid people with their stapled stomachs and guns are watching Fox News and learning real good from human carrion like fat, limp-penised druggie Rush Limbaugh (caught returning from a weekend in the Dominican Republic, celebrated Sex Tourism Central, with a bottle of Viagra with someone else's name on it—who had to service him? At least the woman who slept with British Deputy PM John Prescott got £100,000 for her story. What will some Dominican hooker get? Crushed, I'd say) and that ignorant bloated lump of rage Bill O'Reilly and that's all there is to say, there's nothing more.

Americans can't even do anger properly. People they disagree with are harpy millionaires enjoying their husbands being burned to death in the Twin Towers on September 11, 2001. Or so says Ann Coulter. They can't even do insults properly. Whereas the British do it right. Charlie Brooker wrote of Bush, "Where's Lee Harvey Oswald when you need him?" No more need be said. Of course it was the Americans who got upset. About a man whose presidency was nothing but telling lies and torturing people, while tapping their phones and prodding their bank accounts. I swear, they only objected because Oswald killed Kennedy, and Kennedy and Clinton were the only do-able U.S. presidents in history. How low this country has sunk.

Go to hell, America. I couldn't have dreamed a more awful place if I'd tried. I wish the Stay-Puft Marshmallow Man would just sit on your country and squash you all into a seat cover. I can see the globules popping out at the edges, arcing into the Atlantic and Pacific, the waters rising with this new mass to accommodate.

Do it soon. Do it now.

Things I Like About Americans

Let's get personal here

The greatest thing Americans have given to the world is rock 'n' roll. I'm going to be very strict in this chapter. I will not point out the irony of the blues that came out of the South being born of black suffering. It's a fact, but many people have suffered and they haven't come up with anything that resonated with humans the way the blues do.

The blues were stolen by whites and in the beginning misused very badly. But the truth is that when I need music to set me on fire or to soothe my soul, I turn mainly to Americans. R.L. Burnside, Billie Holiday, black gospel choirs, Patsy Cline, Southside Johnny and the Asbury Jukes, Patti Scialfa, Carole King, Neil Diamond, the Four Tops, The 4 Seasons, Aretha Franklin, Steve Earle, Ray Charles, Carly Simon, Willie Nelson, Little Richard, The O'Jays, Roy Orbison, Elvis Presley, Kurt Cobain, Muddy Waters, Aerosmith, Louis Armstrong, Dionne Warwick, Emmylou Harris, James Taylor, The Supremes, Paul Simon, Talking Heads, Eric Carmen, Madonna, Buddy Holly, Pete Seeger, Macy Gray, Woody Guthrie, Dinah Washington, Linda Ronstadt, Lucinda Williams, Meat Loaf, Blondie, Etta James, Marvin Gaye, Otis Redding, Tracy Chapman, Bob Dylan, Boz Scaggs, R.E.M, Tina Turner, and you got it, Bruce Springsteen.

And of course there are writers to admire: F. Scott Fitzgerald, Edith Wharton, Anne Tyler, Erica Jong, Anne Sexton, Mark Twain, James Dickey, Jonathan Franzen, Peter Gent, Sue Kaufman, Irwin Shaw, Jean Kerr, Laurie Colwin, Larry McMurtry, Annie Proulx, Anne Lamott, Tom Wolfe, James Baldwin . . .

And the journalists—Barbara Ehrenreich, Seymour M. Hersh, Matthew Brady, Mary Ellen Mark, Susan Sontag, Martha Gellhorn, Barry Lopez, Hunter S. Thompson, E.F. Stone, Helen Thomas, W.E. DuBois, Lincoln Steffens . . .

But you see what is happening here. Not only am I merely compiling lists, but the lists are dwindling. A nation isn't defined by its best people, it's defined by how it treats its most unfortunate people.

Oh dear. We seem to be headed back into the previous essay.

Americans praise themselves, and were once praised, for their freedoms, but they seem to have given them up with little protest and even less noticing. That avenue is gone for me. If we're talking freedom, I have found Europe most pleasant. I have had unfortunate encounters with French doctors and waiters, though never with their gendarmerie. But I am afraid even to try to cross the U.S. border. Forget freedom.

Americans dance well. By that I mean they're not afraid to dance. And they like to drink. Although puzzlingly, not at Christmas. This may be because many of the relatives departed after their Thanksgiving holiday, held alarmingly close to Christmas, and so there is no need to drink heavily at Christmas. We don't even want to discuss the Brits on drinking. So I will praise American good times. So many Hollywood movies take place at parties and gatherings, out at the lake or at baseball games, or around the family dinner table, a place where appetites go to die. For Americans are social, and I am social, although I don't indulge that inclination. The instant friendliness of Americans is very attractive. I've always said there's no better place to have a car accident. There you lie quietly bleeding by the side of the road. Someone is guaranteed to stop and help. It was certainly true in the case of Stephen King, forced to chat with the man who ran him over, but that doesn't say good things about alcohol, so we'll drop that anecdote.

Americans are friendly people. Even when you dislike them, as you frequently do when you're on holiday

(I don't want to talk to people on holiday; that's why I went on holiday), they don't get your barbed remarks. A Canadian's barbed remarks are so sheathed they're almost ungettable, but even a blatant suggestion that the American should go away quietly will go right over an American's head. They're literal. Sometimes it's annoying. Sometimes it charms the hell out of you.

So at this point, Americans are drinking and saying friendly things and dancing to the best rock 'n' roll on the planet. We are doing well in our quest to define our love of Americans.

Americans are tall. This is said to be good. I don't really care how short or tall anyone is, but you know, a long tall drink of water of a human being is an attractive thing. I'm not sure it's good for the planet, though. I bought a Montauk armchair. It never occurred to me that furniture designed for Americans might not fit into the small ecologically friendly house I live in. The chair is so massive it has to have its own room. We even placed a beautifully embroidered wall hanging behind it to create a sense of occasion, as opposed to a sense of "they shoved this armchair into the front hallway because it was the only empty space they had." I enjoy sitting in the chair, but am a little lost in it. It's too far from the TV to be useful, and I always feel as though I am waiting for an uninvited guest, one of those friendly Americans possibly, who will show up with a pie still warm from the oven.

When I bake a pie

For the apple of my eye

I bake it with a crust

I know I can trust.

Tastes so good you can

Smell it from the yard.

Tell you what my secret is

My secret is my lard.

This is my memory of what Loretta Lynn sang in Crisco commercials in the seventies (I must have the lyrics wrong, surely). I suppose the Crisco people were desperate to shift the Crisco image away from its use as a lubricant, but I'm not sure that was necessary. For one thing, any unguent will do. But also, Canadians don't use lard in their pies. They use butter or margarine.

Anyway, I had this image of a nation of madly happy pie-bakers. This image finally came true in the nineties with the great Martha Stewart, who I defend to this day as a woman who brought good looks and good taste to the home. She restored domesticity, which had had a bad rap since the Second World War. American dining had been deteriorating thanks to the machinations of what I call Big Food (it accompanies Big Pharma in my list of evil cartels). When I say good taste, I mean mouth taste.

That woman's food tastes good. Her homes look good and are cared for with a precision I admire. You can bet her white picket fences aren't made of plastic. When she does a domestic task, she does it right. When she cheats on the stock market, she does it wrong. Still.

I said earlier that Americans are tall. They like bigness in all respects, and no, this is not a dig at their weight. They like life on a large scale. The Grand Central Oyster Bar in New York City is a marvellous place. The problem is, the oysters are terrible. All the food at this huge gorgeous gigantesque luncheonette is horrible, except for the tea biscuits. I gobble those tea biscuits. Anything but the sole à la meunière. How do you ruin a sole? You leave it around dead for quite a while, I'm thinking.

So America is good at grand gestures. On the details, not so much. This makes Martha Stewart un-American, but I suspect she is. She has a sternness to her, such a high bar of accomplishment, which blocks her from the world of foodies. Julia Child was highly skeptical of Stewart perfectionism. On Stewart's Christmas special on which Child was a guest, Stewart's dessert was a ginger-bread house of her own house, of all things. Stewart did that sugar-spinning thing and Child marvelled. "Aren't we terrific?" she said. Snicker from the audience. Child was a sensualist, Stewart an overachiever.

Nevertheless, Stewart set a standard in a country that makes its own standards, low and heading lower. It can only be a good thing. I could watch Martha all day, doing the things I'll never do. I've been planning to paint my interior window frames in semi-gloss white for a decade now. One day it might happen.

I'm not listing again, am I? Martha Stewart is something of a list all her own.

Americans are generous. I suppose that may be because they have money, but fewer Americans have money now and they're still generous. The British upper classes are stingy as hell. Canadians cannot begin to understand the concept of the *lagniappe,* the unexpected gift. The Japanese prefer the expected gift . . . Look, I'm descending into racial stereotypes here. Americans are generous, easygoing people. I've said enough.

They're also a clean people, or were, and this mattered a great deal to me. I cannot tell you how much I admired it. Now that I have my own house, and probably since I reached the age where my sweat began to smell, I've been aware of genuine cleanliness and how hard it is to achieve. Americans once had gleaming vitreous china in their bathrooms, their dining room serving platters sparkled and their laundry was a national fetish.

This has changed. Corporations changed it with their mania for the lowest possible price. I don't necessarily think the lowest possible price is the best possible price, not if the hotel room no longer offers facecloths, the coffee maker is in the bathroom, of all places, and the whole set-up looks a bit . . . worn. I remember seeing a large chip of plastic sealant/paint that had come off the frame of an airline seat on Northwest Airlines ten years ago and thinking, no decent international airline would do that. They would and they did. Now Air Canada offers me hard, chipped seats, junk food for a price, blankets covered with human hair and, worst of all, no heavy-duty paper towelling on the headrests. I'm amazed we don't all have lice.

The theme is, I suspect, that the things I love about Americans are being betrayed. That nation has lost so much to the corporation. That's why it's pleasing to see

American corporations sag, to the benefit of everyone including its citizenry. Here's the most pathetic example.

A proposed merger is in the works involving General Motors and Renault and Renault's affiliate Nissan. David Olive, an accomplished Canadian business writer, explained what that meant. GM, he said, the people who created Chevrolet, Pontiac, Buick and Cadillac, now sees its Chevrolet division valued at the same amount as America's second-ranked mouthwash. That's Listerine.

The great American journalist David Halberstam wrote a book about GM's humiliating decline. It was called *The Reckoning*. The problem is, it was published in 1986. This means GM had twenty years to fix itself and it didn't. While Toyota was making well-designed and hard-wearing cars at low prices, GM was looking to the short-term, turning out cheapo gas-guzzling SUVs at zero-percent financing. They were paying Americans to buy their cars. No one else was going to buy crap like that.

Once again, I name something about America I like and it turns out to be a pale shadow of its former self. In this case, it's a fine, albeit belated, blessing for the environment. But still . . .

So I ask an American friend living here with her Canadian husband what she loves about her country. She responds by e-mail after several days' thought. "I love that American quarters are big enough so that I can differentiate quarters and nickels."

I can't even give her name. She works for the U.S. federal government and Homeland Security is already keeping an eye on me. Let's just call her Valerie Plame.

She adds the standard qualifier: "Right now, I like that I don't have to live in America . . . just visit sometimes."

Thanks, Val.

Pieces of Cake

Yes, there are consolations

 Your home is your nest. It's your Howards End. Stay inside it when you feel small. Venture out when you're feeling tall, knowing you can always flit back to the nest.

Be a perfect aunt. There are no perfect mothers, but aunts can manage it. The pleasures of being a magnificent aunt, a giver of gifts, a praiser of nieces, cannot be quantified. But I know that the heart expands. If you are an imperfect niece, I congratulate you. Your aunts will still adore you.

—

Everything that has gone wrong in the Western nations was caused by Rupert Murdoch, the introduction of air conditioning into the American South and the triumph of plastic over metal, wood and stone. This will end, perhaps not in time, but it will end.

In 1998, the famously self-effacing British writer Alan Bennett was offered an honorary doctorate at Oxford University. He turned it down, telling Oxford that if the university thought it was appropriate to establish the Rupert Murdoch Chair in Communications, why not approach Saddam Hussein to found a chair in Peace Studies. Bad money for good ends is all very well, Bennett wrote, but there's a limit. Reading this, I found it noble and wonderful by any measure. And such gestures are easy to make. Yet almost no one makes them.

Ferragamo court shoes are excellent and will last. There is much goodness in buying well-made shoes. Cheap shoes are false economy.

Not so with purses. A big well-designed lightweight nylon purse with a central zippered compartment and flat shoulder straps is all you need. If you ever find such a purse, buy five. It took me decades to learn this; you have it for the price of a book.

Venice is overrated. Paris is not. Many will disagree but it is the weight of tourists that is making Venice sink and perhaps this judgment will help a little with that. Also,

Venice is a stage set. People actually live in Paris. They're quite disciplined about it.

Men look best in dark suits, white (or pink) shirts with spread collars and elaborately patterned ties. All else is dross. You know this is true. Mmm, baby. How glorious is a man in a good-looking suit.

The most soothing thing in the world is to give all your extra money to Amnesty International. Somewhere, somehow, while you are doing the dishes or going on with your doggy life, your money is offering balm to a thin, frightened bleeding person you will never know of and never meet.

As Loretta Lynn once suggested about what she called the "deely-bob," I do think the clitoris should have been placed closer to the opening of the vagina. How about in the vagina? Still, one does one's best with given placement, and one's best is often quite spectacular.

When I pay my dues, the Writers' Union of Canada sends me a small certificate declaring me to be a Member in Good Standing. Think of that. With whom else are you in good standing for an entire year? How many people? Institutions? Bosses? I regularly fall out even with magazines I subscribe to. The Writers' Union fees are cheap at any price, I say. If only all harmonious relations were so easily obtained.

—

The happiest times of my life are when I'm horizontal. On the bed, mainly, and after that, the couch. Couchettes on trains. Lying on the floor with an infant. This differentiates me from those lively people who walk, visit, barge in, wave their arms at parties and make a new friend of the person whose head has just been doused with their drink, and those people who hit European cities running when they arrive jet-lagged at their hotel and the room isn't ready for five hours, rather than pester the front desk, shout and drape themselves on the couch in the lobby looking like death until the hotel relents. I used to be one, now I'm the other. It's just another version of happiness. Standing up, lying down, same difference.

Please go away. I do not wish to see you again. Do not call me. The point in a woman's life when she is able to say these things to men and women she wishes to banish— now that's called being grown up. I am a grown-up. My youth is gone, I have traded the bloom for gloom, but being able to state the facts without blinking is worth it.

I have had many moments, days, even years, of huge happiness in my life when I have entirely forgotten myself. It causes me great pain to remember this. I would give almost anything to be able to relive those times. The great writer on depression, Andrew Solomon, goes even further. It is past happiness that gives him greatest pain. I don't go quite that far. The fact that the future's ahead of me and may contain more of those marvellous times that I will remember with anguish is a comfort.

—

No dish is finer than a lobster served with vanilla sauce. This is not widely known. Seek it out. Eat it often.

There is nothing wrong with your face that T. LeClerc Poudre Éclat can't fix. Many mornings have I tested this thesis and re-proved it each time.

One shot of vodka (once a day) will cure what ails you. My friend Henry taught me this.

Children should not spend too much time with their parents. They should be with friends, playing, or off on their own, living inside their own heads. I look at the parents of my friends and think, "That raised you?" Parents are as damaged as anyone else. Their children should be given a fighting chance. So come on over to my house. Children give me great delight.

I become aroused (it isn't exactly sexual, but it is a body-and-brain pleasure) in foreign bookstores. I breathe hard and look around in vain for a grocery cart to load up the goods. In my own country, I simply feel unsettled in bookstores. Odd people populate them, as they do the postal service. Is this normal? Presumably London gourmands feel the same way in Barcelona's Boqueria market, but yawn at specialty shops in Holland Park. My point is the heart beats faster at many things, not just a cigarette with a lipstick's traces.

—

My dream is to travel somewhere where no one knows me. Where I am completely free. But inevitably, you run into people who live one street over and greet you effusively though you would scarcely bother saying hello at home. I am hoping Japan will do the trick. The language is beyond me, the food is frightening, the architecture and all daily matters are entirely unfamiliar.

If they never published another book, we would always have Shakespeare and of him you will never tire. He's bread, he's water, he's champagne, he's cake, all in one. Shakespeare would never have expected to be the most talented and famous writer (and book-title provider) of his species. There's nothing stranger than imagining him on a typical day, washing his face, having his hose mended, scribbling away . . . and being unaware of his life after death. Imagine that.

And finally, I give you my choice. No, it's not death. That choice has been made for me, you see. And you too. Sorry, did you not grasp that? We will eventually die.

Choose cake, I said at the beginning. And here is the cake I choose. I have been baking it all my life: Ambrosia Chiffon Cake, taken from Cake Secrets: Unveiling the Joyous Mysteries of the Loveliest of Cakes, a pre-feminist housewives' pamphlet from a flour company in the 1950s. It hung around the house until I left home in 1977 with a photocopy. I assume the original cake scientists are dead now. They were a bit nutty but they knew their cakes.

Oh, you can have your butter cakes, your sponge cakes and your angel food cakes, but nothing surpasses the true chiffon. The basic frostings are seven-minute, uncooked butter, quick cooked and boiled, but I don't think you can do better than messing around with cream. That's *heavy* cream. It's cream that means business.

Here is my recipe for Ambrosia Chiffon Cake. Have your measured ingredients to hand so as to avoid panic. While the upside-down cooling period may be alarming, all will go smoothly if you follow the instructions. If you are impatient, as I tend to be, and the cake falls out of the tin in a sort of wet sag, do not scoop the sadly uncooked batter with your bare hands and throw it at the kitchen window in a rage, weeping with anger, as I have. I didn't give the cake a chance to dry and firm up. And I blame the harshness of the laws of gravity. They are implacable. Best to eat the batter raw and try again another day.

AMBROSIA CHIFFON CAKE

Preparations. Let the eggs stand at room temperature an hour or two before using. Have ready an ungreased 8-inch square pan. Start the oven for moderate heat (350°F/180°C). Sift flour once before measuring.

1 cup plus 2 tablespoons sifted cake flour	280 mL
1 1/2 teaspoons baking powder	7 mL
3/4 cup sugar	175 mL
1/4 cup salad oil (Mazola or Wesson Oil)	50 mL
2 free-range egg yolks, unbeaten	
6 tablespoons water	90 mL

1 tablespoon grated orange rind	15 mL
1/2 cup shredded coconut	125 mL
1./2 teaspoon vanilla	2 mL
1/2 cup free-range egg whites (4 to 5)	125 mL
1/2 teaspoon salt	2 mL
1/4 teaspoon cream of tartar	1 mL

The Mixing Method. Measure sifted flour into sifter, add baking powder and sugar, and set aside. Measure into mixing bowl the oil, egg yolks, water, orange rind, coconut and vanilla. Sift in dry ingredients. Beat 1/2 minute at low speed of mixer, or 75 strokes by hand.

Beat egg whites, salt, and cream of tartar with egg beater or at high speed of electric beater until mixture will stand in *very* stiff peaks—about 3 minutes (The egg whites should be beaten stiffer than for meringue or angel food.) Do not under-beat.

Fold egg yolk mixture thoroughly into egg whites with a large spoon, flat wire whip or rubber scraper. Do not stir or beat.

Baking. Pour batter into pan. Bake in a moderate oven (350°F) for about 30 minutes. A cake tester should come out clean. Cool cake in pan, upside down, for 1 hour, resting corners of pan on two other pans or two full tin cans of equal size. To remove, loosen cake from sides of pan with knife and gently pull out.

Serving. Split cake horizontally. Spread with Ambrosia Cream and coconut.

AMBROSIA CREAM

2 tablespoons icing sugar	30 mL
1 cup heavy cream	250 mL
1 teaspoon vanilla	5 mL
1/4 teaspoon almond extract	1 mL

Combine ingredients in bowl. Chill thoroughly. Then beat until cream will hold its shape. Pile lightly over middle and top layers of cake. Makes 2 cups (500 mL). Scatter with coconut shreds. The cake should be refrigerated after serving. It tastes even better cold.

Acknowledgments

The woman who accompanied me through the past two years was the great Anne Lamott, whose memoirs and essay collections kept me going until I discovered her novels, and then I rolled about in clover.

To my women friends, my pit crew, I offer thanks: Jennifer (Jinks) Hoffmann, Jennifer Lanthier, Michelle Quance, Lee-Anne Goodman, Fiona Sampson and Marilyn Churley. Thank you, Liz Clarkson, friend of my youth; Rosanna Serpa, friend of my youthiness and doctor of my hair at the Disegno salon in Toronto; and Pam Davies, friend from the peculiar years. Kristine Quan grew up next door; I wish I had been a better friend despite the distance of a driveway. I honour her beauty, her courage, and her escape. Thank you, Dr. Henry Morgentaler, for enhancing all our lives, but mainly for taking me out to lunch once a month and always paying. Thanks to Mary Sheppard, Naomi Klein, Michele Landsberg, Avi Lewis, Sylvia Stead, Sara Angel, Cindy Brown, Angela Cavanagh, Jamie Donaldson, Joyce Guest, Anne Kingston, and Andy Strote.

My friends Buzz and Tennyson always welcome me and I am flattered senseless. Thank you, Stephanie, Ethan, Nicola and James. For allowing me into the family, I thank Samantha and Victoria, my beauties, my treasures, my great hope for old age (but don't forget to pull the plug, darlings). For putting up with a mad auntie, thank you, blithe Sarah, and a special thanks to Alexandra for her sense of wonder, her gaiety and her fragrant wraparound hugs. Thanks, Hazel, for letting me borrow your girls. My love for my mother, Laura, is beyond words.

I used to find it odd when people thanked their agents, thinking it was just a money deal. It's not. Bruce Westwood has been a generous friend and wise adviser. He is a great enjoyer and enhancer of life.

Michael Schellenberg, my editor at Knopf Canada, was cheerful and encouraging when I was at my most Eeyore-ish. His advice and Jamie Kennedy lunches were invaluable. Consider it done, Michael. Louise Dennys was patience incarnate, always encouraging to this itchy yet apologetic writer. Thanks also to wonderful Amy Maclin at the New York Times Syndication Service who improved my columns—all insulting her president—without hurting my feelings, no easy task, and her boss Michael Oricchio, who I will meet in better times, I hope. And I still miss you, Diane Turbide.

Thanks to Mil Millington and Charlie Brooker for kindly giving permission for me to quote them.

Profound thanks go to Lawrence and Andrew at Firesnacks, who came racing to the house like paramedics after I deleted the book.

I had company on the trail. Blue Rodeo, Bruce Springsteen and Kate Bush stayed with me as I wrote. Linwood Barclay, Stephen Colbert, Eddie Izzard, John Hodgman, Mark Morford, Matthew Norman, Deborah Ross, Alexei Sayle, Sandra Shamas, Jon Stewart, Rebecca Tyrrel, and Red Green kept me laughing. Noam Chomsky and Robert Fisk kept me honest. Doris Lessing, Joan Barfoot, and Helen Simpson kept me intimidated.